I0790575

Back to Life, Back to Reality

CARL W. MOHLER, JR.

authorHOUSE

AuthorHouse™
1663 Liberty Drive
Bloomington, IN 47403
www.authorhouse.com
Phone: 833-262-8899

Published by AuthorHouse 04/14/2021

ISBN: 978-1-6655-2297-7 (sc)
ISBN: 978-1-6655-2301-1 (e)

Print information available on the last page.

Any people depicted in stock imagery provided by Getty Images are models, and such images are being used for illustrative purposes only. Certain stock imagery © Getty Images.

This book is printed on acid-free paper.

Contents

Introduction vii

I.   The Beginning I Didn't Want 1

II.   The Introduction of a New Chore.....................10

III. I am the Bolo King......................................16

IV. The Struggle at Home..................................23

V.   A Complete Turn Around 35

VI. Marching Forward to Germany 58

VII. I Didn't Deserve This.....................................68

VIII. The Horror Continues 78

IX. One More Chance 85

X.   The Final Countdown.................................98

Introduction

I must be the indecision king. Sometimes the toughest decisions to me are made completely easy by someone else's gentle touch. In this case, it was my dental hygienist who led me down the path of becoming a complete intellect again, after an almost full recovery from an illness known as viral encephalitis, which is an injury to the brain, that may be fatal. I wanted to blame myself for every negative decision, but after an eight-year struggle in which my life had nearly been ended by encephalitis and the traumatic brain injury it caused, I wonder "Why me?". It is really almost too hard to explain unless you have had to live it day in and day out.

My intelligence is something that I used to really take for granted, even with the bipolar illness. However, 2015 really made me rethink whether I should continue down that path. Writing this book was made significantly easier after sitting in the dentist's chair for thirty-five minutes. Instead of worrying about my teeth (she did her job), the hygienist challenged my intellect by driving me to recapture the events that I needed to share with the rest of the world, so that they would have a firm understanding of what it was like to live on the intellectual edge.

Since I wrote my first personal novella, *Moving Beyond What I Left Behind*, I have taken the time to reflect as to where my trials and tribulations with the bipolar illness may have actually begun. I never knew what motivated me to do what I did when I was in my early adult years, but sometimes things happen. I guess I got away with the immature stuff I did because everyone in my peer group was rather immature themselves at that point in time. My assumption was that the bipolar illness had never been diagnosed at that point in time. Either there was not a true professional in my academic surroundings who was capable of diagnosing whether I was bipolar or not, or it had not manifested itself to the point where I had come across as truly being bipolar. At that point in my life, I also didn't have the worldly experience to know if I had a mental illness or not.

Just to recapitulate from my first novella, the bipolar disorder used to be more commonly known as manic depression. It is a serious mental illness that can lead to risky behavior, discharged relationships, ended careers, and potential suicidal tendencies, if it is not effectively treated. I think I have traveled down those roads on several occasions and somehow survived. Bipolar disorder is characterized by extreme changes in mood from mania, an extreme high, to depression, an extreme low. In my experience, the great majority of the time I have normal behavior patterns, as long as I stick to my medical treatment plan. 2000 to 2007 were incredibly positive years; then 2008 to 2014 were rebuilding years. With God's speed, 2015 forward will be years that only the most powerful intellects can imagine.

Now that I reflect back on all the issues I had to deal with as a young person living with the bipolar personality, I can definitely reflect in fear as narcissistic traits developed in me as I grew up. These traits can be associated with a personality disorder in which the person has a distorted self-image, is unstable, and has intense emotions. There were many times in which I may have been overly preoccupied with vanity, a false prestige, power, and a sense of personal inadequacy. There were points in which I really lacked empathy towards other people, and I had an exaggerated sense of superiority. There were times in which I really didn't care about life itself or other people's feelings. Over time these traits became manifested by my struggles with Post Traumatic Stress Disorder or the bipolar illness. This just made me feel more inadequate about myself in the long run.

As I was revisiting the pain that haunted me in college, because at that time I had not been diagnosed as being bipolar, I felt like I was the definition of narcissistic without even trying to be. I had to boost my own ego by enrolling in all the top classes, which for some God-forsaken reason made me feel like I was intellectually superior to all my classmates. I was smart enough to fool myself without even trying. To my chagrin, I had successfully withdrawn from all these classes to pursue a more liberal arts degree in History. I am not going out on a limb here and saying history was a fluff subject, but I had priorities, and my priority was to maintain a certain GPA for my scholarship in ROTC. I didn't know I was bipolar at the time, but all the clues were there to indicate that I was.

I failed my first round of exams in Analysis and Chemistry. When I asked ROTC if I could change my degree to History and maintain my scholarship, they didn't object. The issue of being bipolar had never surfaced at that point. I was too naïve to raise this issue, and I didn't question anybody's ethics about how I was being treated.

The first thing to remember is that my illness had not manifested itself to the point that the professionals constantly grooming me could detect it, even if they had known what they were looking for. I think they might have been operating under a rather bold assumption that anybody who could graduate from basic training should be "good to go" in the ROTC program. Also, as far as the professionals went, they just saw a young cadet grow with every professional encounter, except for when I lost a compass on a field training exercise.

It was an obsession for me to improve to become the best cadet I could be, and there were times I excelled above the rest. I never wasted an opportunity to make my college look good in training, and I learned everything I could about what the Army had to offer. I thought I was becoming the ultimate at what I did, and I thought I would professionally excel in the future, until I went to Fort Bragg for Advanced Camp. My dream quickly turned into a disaster.

One of the toughest obstacles I ever had to overcome was self-medicating with alcohol and being obsessive-compulsive at the same time. I had never had a drink before I went to college. I was only 19 when I went to a party that practically took me to the edge. At that point I found out beyond a shadow of a doubt that I had a devil inside of me, which was consuming me. I didn't even realize what I was doing to myself. The drinking just made me feel incredibly good the next morning, as if I hadn't been abusive the previous night. Ironically, the military pushed me to be more of a man than ever before. For some reason I used that as an excuse to drink more and more as I matured into manhood.

As the bipolar illness began to erupt in my life, it laid the groundwork for me to become an alcoholic, even though I didn't realize it. Every time I had some type of a mood swing, I escaped reality by drinking. I didn't know if friends sensed there was something wrong or not, or if, like everyone else, I was just drinking to escape reality. When I was in Europe, I would be in the club night after night throwing money away, thinking I was just reliving the fun of my college years, when in all reality, I was trying to escape a hidden evil inside of me. I was destined for failure in the military; I just would not openly admit to myself that my abusive lifestyle was the cause of it. I was grandiose in my thinking, and no challenge was too big or too small. I knew I had issues at this point, but I was completely forlorn and at a loss for common sense. The days were dominated by pain and ups and downs. My evenings were left in suffering by the insanity of self-medication. I think the thing that really helped me pull it together for the short term after I left the Army was all the individual role models I confided in about my mental illness and who made me promise to quit drinking throughout my endeavors in life. My word was my bond. It has carried me for over the past fifteen-plus years to success in one shape, form or another.

Even though I attempted to find a new identity for myself when I first left the military, I struggled to find a professional life for myself. I thought I deserved to pick up where I left off in the service. I was in for a rude awakening. I ended up just roaming from one factory to the next while I waited for my chance to go back to school and retrain. In 1992, if my memory serves me correctly, I was oh so politely informed I was bipolar, which meant absolutely nothing to me. I didn't take the initiative to research what the bipolar illness was. Even if I had, I don't think I would have believed the research, other than saying this can't be happening to me. Self-denial is an easy way out when you are bipolar. I was denying my whole existence at that point. Why, I don't know, but I was totally rebellious at that point in my life. For many reasons, I just wanted to be anti-social. I was willing to spend my money in that fashion as well. I lived only to damage myself. My self-esteem was at an all-time low. I was in a downward spiral which almost drove me to the point where I conceivably wanted to end my life. I was so enriched with everything to offer, yet I just wanted to end it all. My medication was not strong enough; it left my head spinning every day. The constant chaos in my life got me to write a suicidal letter to the Lebanon VAMC, which got me placed on a lockdown ward for about five weeks. I was introduced to Tegretol and a new world of psychotherapy, which started to boost my morale and help stabilize my mood. Once I got my wits about me and showed my grit and determination, I got my ticket punched to get my second bachelor's degree in business management.

My first and only thought when I applied to go back to school was that I was going to get my teaching certification in Secondary Education Social Studies. Quite the wrong answer. I took an aptitude test. To my misfortune I entered into an agreement with the VAMC to go back to school for Business Management. The VAMC's first requirement for me was to get motivated and get my life back on track. So, I got motivated by Army standards and got a real job by Lancaster County standards. Everything in that combination seemed to be ideal, including the pseudo social life I seemed to have going for myself.

Halfway through the completion of my degree, I was employed at a local bank as a financial sales representative when the bipolar illness lifted its ugly head one more time. Any little negative event would cause me to break out in tears; I would go hide in a back room to hide my emotions. My boss was less than ideal. I had never been harassed by a woman before, but it was happening. She didn't understand why I shut her out emotionally during the workday, but I didn't know how to handle her overzealous and forward behavior. To make a long story short, Human Resources dismissed her for harassment and other issues. Four months later I decided to seek employment elsewhere because my bipolar illness was a negative issue to me again, and nobody else really understood what the illness entailed.

I couldn't imagine what employment would be like after I left the bank. I looked high and low. Then it came to me in the form of working as an inside sales account manager for a high-tech manufacturer of copper and fiber optic wire. This was another job in which I was not destined to be level-headed, thanks to my bipolar side, and my degree of professionalism was not destined to work out well with my employer or my fellow workers. This really put a strain on my personal relationships as well. I thought my personal relationships with my family members and close friends were really balanced, but perhaps I was thinking too much at that point. I didn't completely understand what I was going through because I had no firm grasp as to what being bipolar was all about. I really did have a high appreciation of my job, but a lot of people in the corporate structure were greatly angered by my inability to deal with my professional and personal issues. Granted, this was almost 25 years ago, but that was a growing pain I wish I hadn't had to go through because, as I mentioned before, I did find a high degree of enjoyment in my job. The company had faith in me because they gave me a degree of financial assistance toward my Master's degree, but unfortunately the bipolar disorder was more than I could handle at that point in time, and somehow, my boss directly reinforced that fact. I could rise to the occasion to compete at the same level as the other employees, but I had a problem, and my boss didn't hesitate to make the best decision she could possibly make for the company and for me. Even though I was faced with unemployment, I wasn't ready at that point to give up on my professional career.

My professional career quickly took me from the country area of Mohns to Malvern PA, which is a suburb of Philadelphia. Needless to say, I was in awe by just the extreme magnitude of my new work environment. I thought I had found the dream job of my choice as a cost accountant. The salary was excellent, the benefits were awesome, and my new boss was fabulous. The only thing that didn't work for my new boss was when he found out something was wrong with me. I had tried everything to maintain professional decorum at work, but bipolar patients are excellent at making fun of anyone who I felt was inferior to me, or old. I really didn't pay attention to my own behavioral problems.

As a cost accountant, my job was to maintain accountability of the inventory from the time it came into the door, went into production, and out the door as a finished product. The company had had some issues with their cash stream for several months because my memory wasn't working very well at tracking inventory through the system. I won't blame this one on anyone else, but I could not multitask very well while my mind was in a manic state. I came across well as a person, but in the corporate climate I was nothing short of being a wreck. The controller was a perfectionist who wondered why he had hired an MBA student from my school. His decision was quick; I didn't fault him whatsoever for firing me. I survived, and I moved on. I didn't fault him for not understanding I was bipolar. My illness was beyond his control, but I lived to write about it and make life better for myself once again.

I always had to keep striving on, no matter what the cost. My next stop was the bank where I worked as a financial systems analyst. I thought I was the hotshot MBA from the local university and that any temp agency would be able to place me at top dollar. I felt it was all going my way until I had a conversation with another employee and confided the fact that I was bipolar. He came across as being incredibly intelligent and claimed he was also bipolar, but I couldn't confirm it. Three weeks into the job, I started having a slight manic swing, and my work habits became slightly unorthodox. I don't know if the bank intentionally fired me for being bipolar, but eventually I had become a distraction to the rest of the workforce, and my personal issues were following me into the office.

As time went on, I could not escape the reality of the momentum. It had to happen: the most feared aspect of the disorder that a bipolar person may have—racing thoughts and information anxiety. In my case, when I have racing thoughts, I can absorb information so quickly that it is enough to drive me to the edge and beyond. The only thing outside of medication that would help was alcohol. Because I wasn't on medication, alcohol was my only alternative. I now cry at this thought, because intelligence was my passion, yet alcohol left me feeling distorted. I couldn't focus or concentrate. My grades began to slip, and I began to panic in my classes. Somehow, I needed to get these particular issues under control because I needed my degree to survive in the corporate jungle. It was my decision to turn in the direction of the VAMC one last time. I realized I needed to make one last tough decision for myself.

I thought I had escaped the world of racing thoughts, but I learned that phenomenon is what makes knowledge a true oblivion. Pure energy raced through my brain at a million miles per hour, and the inspirations I came up with were either extremely efficient and idealistic, or extremely ludicrous. Due to the openness of my heart, one thought that invaded me time and time again was neverending—would I ever be normal. Damn the feelings of my soul.

At that time, I was also very focused on getting a job through the online community with haste. ~~Since~~ Because I was a former officer for the Adjutant General Corps, I thought I could get an online job as the postmaster general for a city out west, even though I was on the east coast. Ludicrous thinking, if you ask me now. However, it was a brilliant idea at the time. I sent a resumé out to California for the job and waited around in my apartment long enough to get a reply that said "Thanks, but no thanks." Finally, I gained some self-control and headed back to the Lebanon VAMC. I was about to approach sanity one more time.

It is very hard for anyone to realize what it was like for me to live in a VA hospital on a lockdown ward while my medical treatment team got me straight and level on medication again. This a tough part to talk about, because I am a highly accomplished member of the academic community and very educated. Most of the tine I spent on that ward was for me to be observed. One night on the ward, I was experiencing racing thoughts. My RN spent time with me while this happened. He convinced me that I needed to buy a trilogy by Dr. Kay Jamison, a noted psychiatrist, who is also bipolar. I became obsessed that my life was a direct reflection of hers. My life mirrored hers in so many ways. She had gone bankrupt and so had I. I didn't plan the bankruptcy—it just happened. She wrote a trilogy, and I had completed a trilogy of novellas. Hers is more medical than mire, whereas mine is more worldly than hers. She is an MD, and I am an ABD, "all but dissertation." I never believed in Déjà vu until I started writing my trilogy. My nurse's nick name was AJ. I don't know if I should say "thank you" or "stay away," because my experience with him has been like a bad nightmare waiting to boil over.

I.

The Beginning I Didn't Want

People with the bipolar disorder usually experience intense emotional states that occur in distinct periods called "mood episodes" (mood liability). These episodes can go from an overly joyful (with excessive laughter) or an excited state (with increased drive) which can lead to destructive behavior called a manic episode. On many occasions, a mood swing is both manic and depressive. People with the bipolar disorder may also be explosive and irritable during a mood swing. On many occasions I had to endure mood swings during which I was very irritable. The trick was in learning how to manage this. Thus, the voyage begins on my personal conflict with the bipolar disorder.

All great fairy tales begin with the words "once upon a time." This one is no exception, from beginning to end. But to put a timeline in place to this odyssey is very difficult. It is also very difficult to make readers understand the growing pains I went through along the way. I found that growing up as a bipolar person can be quite unenjoyable as well. Over the past 27 years the bipolar illness has pushed my personality and stamina to demonic and unreasonable heights without any major notice from people around me, or that was my perception anyway. I always wondered if my perceptions about myself had any value or were true to any degree.

During my childhood and teenage years, mental illnesses were difficult to detect. Special education programs were relatively non-existent prior to the 1990's. I went through my high school and college years unaffected, except for perhaps some mild depression, which I self-analyzed. However, there were some significant factors that accelerated the development of the bipolar disorder. One of them was relocation a good number of times during my school years. Unfortunately, due to poor economic conditions, I was compelled by my parents to move. The move to Pennsylvania was somewhat of an academic shock for me. Despite that, my teachers always encouraged me to fulfill my intellectual gifts and my academic potential. Throughout all my formal years of education, I was allowed to participate in independent studies at all levels, which encouraged my academic gifts and challenged me in every academic level.

Initially, I thought Pennsylvania was going to be a blessing in disguise for me academically, but the move to Pennsylvania was a complete failure and change for me. I let myself down. I don't know howe-I made the decisions as to what subjects I would take, but I replaced Analytical Geometry with Chaucer and Shakespeare. I took Calculus as my sole math class, because I thought that math was going to be my major in college. However, my new love was AP History, which laid the foundation for my future academic achievements in college. However, before considering any college, the first school I wanted to try to apply to was DeVry Technical Institute.

Even though on paper it appeared to be a fit, I didn't like that much of an independent lifestyle that DeVry offered to its students. I liked the students to some extent, and the faculty at DeVry seemed to be very cordial, but I felt too fearful of being in such an open environment. Basically, I felt kind of socially awkward, as if being off the farm for the very first time. I felt that I could not handle that much responsibility at that given point in my life. Also, I had skills tailored for a liberal arts college, not for a technical college. Perhaps I could have mastered the curriculum of the school, but at that point, I didn't think I could excel and apply myself in an urban environment. I was very loyal to my parents. The visit to DeVry made me realize I wanted to be closer to home. New Jersey was like a foreign land to me; I didn't feel I was mentally equipped to do well at DeVry.

My academic years in high school basically prepared me for the college I chose to attend. I thought my background in mathematics had left me well-prepared for a future in math in any college I desired to go to at that point in my life. I was interviewed by Mr. Foster and Dr. Glory, who were in charge of the Math program at the college where I applied, and during the interview, they challenged me to explore new topics and grow beyond my existing boundaries. They had brilliant minds. During the first few weeks of school they helped me discover the new horizons that e college offered, including history. I had never questioned my intellectual gifts in high school, nor did I ever question my abilities to rise up to the new challenges that were being set before me at that point.

These two gentlemen were ~~the~~ intellectual giants and ~~who were~~ the role models I was looking for. I felt positive I had made the right decision in choosing the college I did. After meeting with several other faculty members, I thought I was headed down the right path. I felt this college was my true calling, and I wished I had taken the opportunity to explore my aptitude in other academic fields before then, such as accounting or history.

Oddly enough I began to get frustrated with my personal finances or lack thereof. I felt that I was too good to take a job I felt was demeaning, such as working for minimum wage. However, for the sake of getting drinking money or for supporting my habit of drinking, I did just that. Even though at age 19 I had not yet been diagnosed as bipolar, I started to drink incessantly and worked incredibly hard to support my drinking habits. I didn't know if I was the most aggressive worker food service had, but that time frame is when my aggressiveness started to emerge. I don't want to make any blanket statements about how forward the bipolar disorder made me feel, but I do know I was different from my coworkers. My aggressiveness was to support a habit that would one day potentially kill me, yet it also made me a very energetic person at that point.

After being there only a few short days, I thought the coolest thing on campus was soccer. I had not been recruited to play, but these guys were having a good time chasing the ball around the field, so I figured I could as well. I never had any real skills for sports. Academics—yes. Sports—no. But I was willing to try. I had a positive mental attitude at that point in my life that I could do this at least e once. Then there was a trick to it; the coach asked me to dribble the ball in practice. At this point, the choir was looking all the more attractive. The head coach definitely had some choice words for me. He was fit to be tied when he found out one of his best endurance guys couldn't dribble the ball. I had mastered the technique of having a beautiful short on goal during game warm ups, but during a game it was really unrealistic for me to even attempt a shot on goal. I just didn't have what it would take to be a first-rate soccer player; I think I realized that. I played under every kind of weather condition and realized I was not the man I thought I was. Hell, the coach even asked me to quit before the start of the second season. For some bullheaded reason I refused. I was bound and determined to be the best player I could be, which turned out badly because I really wasn't much of one.

People with bipolar illness are noted to have issues with extremes. I was also very passive-aggressive. Perhaps I was no exception, especially when playing against other players who were extremely aggressive.

Certain players played so aggressively they could have caused bodily harm if they so desired. Sometimes these players would play with exposed metal instruments, which would cause physical damage if the player wanted. The day came on the practice field when it was my opponent and I, one on one. Unfortunately for him—and fortunately for me—I was not going to give him the opportunity to inflict any pain on me. He was a more experienced player than I was, and he was quicker. He had an exposed metal brace with which he came charging at me with a full head of steam. Even though I knew the coach was going to be deeply angered with me later, I did a baseball slide into the player to avoid his exposed knee brace. It was my lucky day to be able to avoid injury, but the coach had a few choice words for me even before practice was over.

From that point forward, the coach saw me negatively, no matter how hard I tried. I over-compensated by lifting weights and doing extra road work. I even started entertaining the notion of playing football. I probably would have gotten annihilated the first day of practice. The first time I lifted weights with the football team, it was a disaster—when I lifted the bar up, the weights fell off both ends of the bar. Grace at its finest.

Football is like anything else you do in life. You must have a knack for playing it; I was about to find out this was something like soccer that I didn't have. However, I was unwavering in the idea that my life was intended for bigger and better things. I was not about to give up until those days arrived.

However, I was destined for bigger and better opportunities.; I just didn't realize it at that time. For a person with the bipolar disorder, "bigger and better" is a very broad term. In my case it meant that I took a few more risks in college than other students. I just felt like I was living beyond my capabilities and pushing my potential to an all new level. My goal was to test life for everything it was worth.

It all started with my academics where I thought I could tolerate the rigors of any topic, from Math to Physics. It took me a solid 10 years after I graduated from college to realize that my true calling was teaching Accounting, and that all my efforts in the hardcore sciences had been in vain.

To support my vanity, for some reason I decided I wanted to pledge a fraternity to see if I could balance out my life and expand my horizons. Most of the guys I pledged with played sports, so I knew we all drank excessively after each game or otherwise when I felt like it. Whether we won or lost, everyone had a blast. We were all friends on Saturday evening, sharing our growing pains. I was going to pledge the fraternity which invited me to pledge and thus open up a month of fun.

I can remember a lot of different pledging nights, but one stood out by itself. I had a chance to play a little football against the meanest and most physically dominant players the football team ever had. I was going to be a real hero 'versus' experience. I have to admit I am not a pretty boy, but for the first time in my life I think I had someone beat in the looks department. I'm going to call this opponent Igor. I was going to prove to him that I could do a bull rush against him. It didn't work. There was a thud and a groan as I tried to pick myself up from the snow. Igor just smirked at me and said, "Pretty boy, huh?" Then as a sign of good will he picked me up from the snow and said, "Find your own glasses, Poindexter." Two weeks later I became a member of the fraternity, thanks to Igor. He is my hero to this day, or so he thinks. However, putting all sarcasm aside, he was always a good guy to hang around with on campus.

During my freshman and sophomore years of college, I really didn't experience too many highs and/or lows because I started to self-medicate with alcohol. To make a long story short, I didn't even know I had a mental illness, but it seemed like I was developing a pattern to keep that illness under control and keep my life consistent and stable. Even though I had pledged a fraternity, I avoided all forms of socialization if at all possible, unless it involved my closest friends, of whom none knew my demonic secret, including myself. Somehow, though, I knew something was wrong. I could feel it manifesting itself inside of me. However, life went on as usual, as long as I continued to drink.

Academically, I was sliding all over the spectrum. Mathematics, Chemistry, Physics—I just couldn't find my niche. After three semesters in college, clearly, I was not doing well. I thought joining the Navy would be my salvation. Eventually I shied away from the pressures of the naval recruiter, thanks to the wily influence of an administrator at college, who persuaded me to stay in school. I found another path which would allow me to excel. I finally found a niche that would see me through to graduation with a high degree of success. I joined the Army Reserves, changed my college major to History, became a supervisor in the food service/ conference service department, and quit playing sports. I definitely was not going to become a professional athlete, so quitting was not a bad option. The only thing I could not seem to shake was the amount of time I spent abusing alcohol. At this point, my drinking had become excessive; I found myself waking up with hangovers three or four mornings a week, including weekends. Unfortunately, I became extremely moody when I didn't drink.

II.

The Introduction of a New Chore

Out of all the concentrations available in the History department, I enjoyed Military History the most because of my experience in the Army Reserves and my exposure to the campus ROTC program. My introduction to the Army Reserves and the Army ROTC program opened up a whole new career field for me. I think for the first time in my life I felt anger about not recognizing this sooner. The Army Reserve was like an introduction to corporate America at a micro level that would pay dividends years later when I went on active duty as a commissioned officer. I even knew that my first paycheck as a lieutenant was going to be substantially more than what I had earned in the Reserves or in ROTC (a motivating factor in itself). Even though I was only a private at the time (at the low end of the pay scale), I knew all my hard work would eventually be rewarding. I wasn't all about hard work, though. I did have a good time jockeying tanks around in the motor pool in the dead of winter. The weekend drill always gave me a reason to drink when I got back to campus, as an outlet for my aggressive behavior.

My overly aggressive behavior was not really apparent to me at this point in time. I do not know what possessed me to want to be involved in barbaric acts such as flesh-piling my friends, but I openly participated if it appeared there was no wrong in the matter, but apparently there was. Years later I would regret the friendships that were lost due to such childish acts.

The next step in my professional military development was basic training for the Army Reserves. My personal objective before I went to basic training was to make myself into the most physically fit private in basic training. I didn't hesitate to overcompensate in the weight room, and I did more road work, so that I maxed my body out even before doing a pushup. I was about to pay a heavy price for this over-compensation in basic training in one way or another. When troops in training environments are moving at a high rate of speed, they are usually put in cattle trucks before being moved to the training areas. Enlisted soldiers learn to save time in the morning by showering at night, because 50 troops in the cattle truck can have a rather odious effect the following morning when preparing to move out to the range or another training area.

Then it came! Day Six, Boys, Love It and Leave It! Welcome to Basic Training, Third Platoon, Rock Platoon, Best Platoon, Rock! Fifty-three privates strong, packed into a cattle truck, moving out at an incredibly high rate of speed for Bravo Company. That is when I should have quit, but I was standing tall and looking good. I should have been in Hollywood. Basic Training is where I met the meanest person in the world, the drill sergeant waiting for me to get off the cattle truck with a very direct order for me to "beat my face," because he thought I was worse than any of the other privates on the truck. His name was Pat Sirois; he was the leanest and meanest "brown round" Chicago had ever had. I flew off that truck so quickly that before I knew it, I was on the dirt doing push-ups ("beating my face") like you wouldn't believe. The man had my number, and he was enjoying every minute of it. Two hours later he found another private to pick on, and I was finished, finished. "God help me if it gets any worse than this," I thought.

Day 2

I shot out of the barracks that morning like greased lightening into the company area. I had never seen such a mean and vicious person wearing a brown round. His name was Joe Simpson. If there was ever a man that could put the fear of God into a new soldier, it was him. He locked me up at the position of attention, looked me square in the eye and said, "Beat your face." After the abuse I had taken the previous day, I thought he was frickin' nuts. Then he looked at me real closely and with a steady sternness, he said, "Private, do you have a problem with communication, or do I have to repeat myself again, 'Beat your face'?"

Not a moment went by where I didn't look at him like he was half loco. I was sizing up Drill Sgt. Simpson as if he were really different. He looked at me one last time and said, "I am going to make myself real clear this time. Drop and give me fifty." That I understood very quickly. Even though I thought the order was a little extreme, I didn't waste any time executing the order. I fully understood what was expected out of me at that point in time. Then my dear Drill Sgt. Ordered me to sound off with my deep impression of lurch with each completed push-up.

Welcome to nine weeks of purgatory in which the whole company formation got to hear me do this three times a day. It was getting to the point where this really wasn't fun anymore. This went on for about two weeks. Then I got introduced to the next phase of basic training, which was going to provide several weeks of pure hell for me.

Week Three, Day 1

The arms room opened at 0645. Mohler with the number 965123. Plastic and metal hit my hands simultaneously. For the first time in two weeks, the fear of weapons was put into me almost instantly. Why I was shaking so much was beyond me, because this was only an M-16 A1 rifle. This weapon had been cleaned and cleared by the armorer before I had even touched it. Nobody in the Army had noticed I was bipolar up to that point, so this week should have been a piece of cake. What did I have to fear except my inability to qualify with a weapon? The Army overlooks things when it comes to meeting a quota, so I can't say I had been taken advantage of at that point. As the old saying goes, "as long as nobody gets hurt, maimed, or killed…," but that didn't change the fact I was really scared of my weapon, and let's face it, what could really go wrong at this stage? How could I not qualify? The numbers, theoretically speaking, were on my side.

Week Three, Day Three

Basic Rifle Marksmanship week was now in full swing. I had learned how to assemble and disassemble my weapon every which way imaginable. Now it was time for the battlefield zero and for me to qualify on the zeroing range. "Assuming the prone position, insert one three-round magazine, place your selector switch on semi, and commence firing. Once you are done firing your weapon, wait to be cleared off the range by a drill instructor. Once the range is cleared, move off down range at a range walk, prepare to zero your target and confirm a battlefield zero." I went to my target and looked and looked. Drill Sgt. Simpson came up behind me, scrutinized my target and said, "Damn, son, what were you aiming at?"

I knew it was going to be a long day. Twenty-one shots later, I still had not zeroed my weapon. Mr. Simpson was beginning to have a serious issue with me. At this point I was beginning to have some grave regrets about enlisting; I wanted to be back in college without delay. I was not in the Infantry, and I definitely was not shaping up to be a great soldier. At zero dark hundred I was the last person to clear off the range, and I was the only private who had not zeroed their weapon yet.

As dusk floated in for the evening, I just hung my head that night in the barracks. It had been an extremely long day that I didn't want to remind myself of or share with anyone else. My roommate, Peter, could see that I was agitated and in a very sober mood. If there was ever a night, I wanted to get a letter from Mom, this was it. She knew I had a hatred for weapons and how focused this part of basic training was. I was only 19 at the time, but I had ambitions to get my doctorate in History, not to kill anybody. However, I was stuck there at the time, so I had to try to make the most out of my position in life, even though I thought this point in my life was being wasted. I smiled inwardly and realized there was always tomorrow, when the qualification challenges would resume. "Oh, woe is me," I thought. I knew I had to succeed the next day. I was not going to accept any excuses out of myself then.

III.

I am the Bolo King

The command echoed in my ears once again. "Lock and load one three-round magazine, place your weapon on semi, and prepare to zero." Once again, I range-walked down the range with Drill Sgt. Simpson to look at my target. He wanted to see the results more than I did. Sure enough, there were three shots almost as tight as a dime dead center on the target. My lessons from yesterday had been well received. Simpson looked at me as if I had accomplished Mission Impossible and then ordered me off the range. I never range-walked so fast as I did at that particular moment. The question of the minute was, would my streak of good luck hold for the rest of the day as I headed towards the qualification range? Drama and suspense were in my mind; I was wondering if I could avoid another negative day.

Range Day One

The sun broke over the horizon as I stared down the firing alley with targets ranging up to three hundred meters away. For some reason I felt this was my day, but I had a degree of self-doubt inside of me. I would have 40 rounds at my disposal to hit 23 targets. The command from the tower echoed out that morning from the officer in charge. He was all business. For some reason I was shaking like a leaf, not knowing if it was due to tremors or if I was really scared. The wartime commands were about to be given. "Firers, assume your fighting position, lock and load one ten-round magazine, place your selector switch on semi, and prepare to defend your position." The word "bolo" echoed in my mind as I squeezed off my first round. I had just defeated my cause before I had even gotten started 40 rounds later, my insights proved to be correct. Drama had pushed me into being the bolo king for the day. (Bolo: failure to qualify with your personal weapon.)

I will refrain from repeating what Drill Sgt. Simpson said to me at that point, when he took his first glance at my score card, other than "Beat your face." My confidence was shot now, but somewhere, somehow, I knew I could pull off this with some effort so I could have success in this segment of basic training like the two hundred other privates who were going to graduate on time.

I was rescheduled to go back to the range the following day. I kept to myself that morning. Everybody in the platoon respected that distance, including Drill Sgt. Simpson. He knew I needed time to myself. I needed to relax and concentrate because this was probably the most important day of basic training for me. If I didn't qualify that day, it would be two days before graduation before I would get to try again. I was just kind of meandering around that morning in the company area when the senior drill approached me and tried to give me a pep talk by saying I wasn't the best, but on the other hand I wasn't the worst he had ever seen. I didn't want to bust this guy's ego right then, but I really wanted to tell him I wanted to be left alone, but he was senior drill, so what could I do about it? How could I tell somebody like that I didn't want to be in another training cycle with him because of some unknown reason called "bipolar" and that somehow, I needed to get back to what is commonly referred to as normalcy. I will admit that these drills are incredibly intelligent men all in all, but outside of the world of the brown round, honestly, they don't have that much going for them. I always had a mutual respect for my brown round, but I always thought his uniform dignified a high level of respect.

Being in basic training was never complete without my mom. I always thought I grew into becoming a solid soldier without her, except when I became slightly hypomanic ~~at one point~~. I called my mother one night, crying and very temperamental, but my mother was not there to answer the phone. She called my Drill Sgt. the following morning and wanted to know why her big private was crying on the phone like I was incredibly homesick. I didn't know why I had done it, because I didn't have an answer about being bipolar.

I had always thought that as a soldier I had it together. However, after I had bolo'd for the third time I had really begun to have my doubts. Then came the day I had really dreaded, the day of the Brigade Commander's inspection. He noticed I didn't have a marksmanship badge on display. I wasn't able to directly look him in the eye and explain why. The Brigade Commander made it really easy on me. He grabbed the barrel of the weapon and showed it to me. I just nodded and waited for him to leave, got out my cleaning kit and went to work on my gun barrel. My name was now mud in the eyes of the Brigade. Life had really taken a downturn in basic training when I had least expected it. I think Drill Sgt. Simpson was really cool about that entire incident. He knew the Colonel had really gotten under my skin that afternoon, but I learned something from the entire scenario besides embarrassment. When my drill Sargent was satisfied that I had cleaned my weapon to standard, he ran me through the entire fundamentals of marksmanship until he was satisfied, I would qualify the next day, hands down. For once I was not afraid of the unknown, because a true professional had instilled confidence in me at his own level, despite my own thoughts of what it would take for me to be successful the following day.

With only a day and a half left until graduation, I was about to find out what it meant to overcompensate. I did everything at a double time, since I wanted to go back to college in the worst way. I was very crisp in every move I executed on the parade field that morning. Standing tall and looking good, I quickly snapped into the position of parade rest when the senior drill approached me. He looked me square in the eyes, as if looks could kill. With ice in his veins, he very directly informed me that if I didn't qualify with my M-16 later that morning, I would be recycled to the next training cycle, meaning not going home, and not going back to college. My ass would be his for another nine weeks. Hostile language usually doesn't work on me, but coming from senior drill that mid-morning, I was starting to shake in my boots a little. I couldn't imagine spending nine more weeks with a royal butthead like him.

It was getting very humid really fast as I loaded my goat-smelling arse on the back end of the company truck midway through the morning. I was a solitary figure on the truck that morning, and I wasn't saying anything to anyone, not even the driver, who was a drill. I think I had even overcompensated on my prayers that morning. I always prided myself in being a thinker, but I wasn't sure how that trait was going to help me that morning. "Brains over brawn, but how?" I asked myself. Then it hit me when I least expected it—psychology. I would use psychology. I had taken psychology in high school. In my case the scorer would be the judge, so I would have to plead my case to the scorer, which was exactly what I intended to do. When we got to the firing range, and I was cleared to enter the range, I wasted no time and went directly to work on the scorer. For some reason he was very empathetic to my case. My drill was confused about what I was thinking and doing. He was very angry that I was not focused on the targets downrange. The officer in charge of the tower took over, and there was nothing more my drill could say. I now had the edge. From that point forward, it was just my scorer and I; My scorer was on my side from that moment on.

"Firers, assume your firing position, lock and load one ten-round magazine, place your selector switch on semi, and prepare to defend your position." After 40 rounds I was cleared off the range with my score card, with my Drill Sgt. trailing a few feet behind. While he waited to review my score card, I did pushups in the sand. He got my score card; the score was 23 out of 40. He was both stunned and livid at the same time. Mr. Sundeen's psychology class from New York Mills High School has bested the top leadership principles from the United States Army. My wit had won the day.

My drill ordered me back on the truck; we hit the road as fast as the old GM could go. As soon as we drove into the company area the drill ordered me off the truck, this time to clean my weapon right. Senior drill wasted no time coming over to see my score card; He called me a lucky SOB. With anger he said, "I will see you tomorrow." I was going to be standing tall and looking good on the parade field one last time. I had beat the Army system with my own form of the buddy system. What a great feeling that was. My reward was getting to march on graduation day. Dressed in class B's, the drill sergeant led the platoons past the reviewing stand.

I had never felt prouder in my professional career than I did at that moment. I felt as if I had really accomplished something worthwhile. I had risen to the challenge of being all I could be, despite the challenges of a disability I was not even aware of. I felt like a million dollars once again.

Just for a moment I was really unsure of myself, and for the first time in basic training I was plagued by confusion. I had initially thought I had wanted to go back to college, but I wasn't sure because the Army had allowed me to escape from the personal confusion and insanity of being in college. Maybe that was meant to be my internal strength. The Army might be the newfound option which would give me energy to keep going, despite my weaknesses. Perhaps if that was an issue, I had addressed two weeks prior to graduation, it would have gone a lot easier for me when it came time to make that decision to go back to college.

While I was momentarily confused, a quick hug from my parents caused me to snap to. I had always been my mother's little boy, but I had a lot of respect for my father as well. However, a quick handshake from a strong-willed Drill Sgt. restored my military bearing very quickly. He gave me a compliment for a job well done, which left me grinning from ear to ear. This was probably the event that made me feel like a real man for the first time in my life.

IV.

The Struggle at Home

Despite this renewed sense of energy and vigor, I was about to go through a period of delayed adjustment when I reported back to college for soccer camp. I wondered if I had even adjusted at all, thanks to the abusive drinking that quickly picked up when I returned to college, but then again, I didn't even know then that I was bipolar. I just felt troubled that I was abusing alcohol to cover everything up, to the extent I was. I used it as a crutch or an excuse to conceal all the negative or inappropriate behavior I had gotten myself involved in. I really became torn in college. I worked extra hard on the field, but I had to keep reminding myself of my three-year ROTC scholarship and its obligations.

Drinking led to my decision to make a change in living accommodations. I had to choose between spending more money than usual to maintain the aloofness of having my own dorm room or moving to a dormitory where social liberties were more aggressive. I decided to interview for a position as a resident assistant in that second type of dormitory, in order to make life a little bit more interesting. I felt that this slight adjustment caused by moving across the street where I could socialize more liberally would somehow keep some of my negative experiences under control. I didn't know if that was the right decision. I didn't want to be overly socializing, but it was an answer that had some appeal.

Narcissism really magnified itself right then. I knew one thing was apparent—that was, if I stayed in the military, I would earn more money, which was what I had done as a private in the Army Reserve. I felt very confident I could excel to new heights if trained properly. That is when the gentleman's world of ROTC entered in the fall of 1986. Soon I was on the verge of another adventure that would lead me to become one of the first two commissioned officers in the history of Lebanon Valley College.

Along with ROTC entering my life, I had to cope with coming home from basic training. The biggest challenge I had was with my aggressive behavior. The complaints began as soon as I got back to campus. It was not only assertive behavior, but I had gone so far as to furnish my dorm room with everybody else's furniture. It was amazing how crooked my room loft had become while I was trying to put it up and drink a six-pack at the same time. I couldn't hit a nail straight if you paid me to. I also wanted to be a hero one last time, so I tried out for the soccer team under a new coach. I made the squad but practicing day in and day out with a hangover did not help my situation any. I had to be everything to everybody, expecting a beer or two in return to satisfy my deepest desires. I knew things were out of control, especially when the Dean of Students called me into his office just to slow me down and advise me that things would be fine. At that point, he did not know I had developed a strong appreciation for Coors Light and that my social life probably would have fallen apart without it.

Things eventually went as the Dean had said they would, except for the drinking issue. My major was agreeable with my academic talents and I liked it. I had a method of paying for college, with a future profession waiting for me after graduation. I was a supervisor in conference/food services, and I belonged to a fraternity without anybody questioning my drinking habits or the fact that I might have an illness except for me. Although this never happened, I wish somebody had been able to tell me I was bipolar. I can't put an exact finger on it, but this time frame was probably about when the illness took root. I had become truly aggressive in my work practices and somewhat defiant. I tried too hard to be socially defiant throughout my growing years and in my work life. Several people started to become concerned, but not me. I was going down the path of self-destruction, but I just didn't realize it.

There were so many different events that transpired during my last four semesters of college that were like escalating factors that increased the likelihood that my condition might take a turn for the worse. What scared me the most, to this day, was that I didn't know I was bipolar, until seven years after my college experience. There were so many different points at which the bipolar illness could have taken a turn for the worse that I can only consider myself to be extremely fortunate things didn't get worse. I am fortunate the binge drinking did not blow up on me y psychologically. It is easy to sit here and apologize to the people who may have been hurt by me throughout the years and may have mixed emotions about me at this point, but I can't gauge the pain and misunderstanding I may have caused friends and families while I was going through my growing pains with the bipolar disorder.

My last two years of college focused around the Reserve Officers Training Corps, classes, and binge drinking. I wanted to let go of the drinking so badly, but I knew if I did, I would be facing almost immediate disaster. From what extreme I didn't know, but at a minimum it would probably mean losing my scholarship and joining Alcoholics Anonymous. Only God would know what catastrophes would emerge at that point as well.

A side aspect of the bipolar disorder is that the patient may exhibit obsessive-compulsive behaviors. I got involved with weightlifting and deadlifting to stay focused—perhaps *overly* focused—at this time in my life.

My drive and desire kept me moving forward until I was deadlifting 500 pounds and bench pressing 295 pounds. I can only guess how much I was squatting then as well. I was continually obsessed to try to push myself harder and harder every day. I worked out with the football team twice a day, plus I was creative enough to invent exercises on my own. I exercised with my friend Igor, who pushed me to my max every day. From day to day, I became more and more exuberant as my abilities to compete at higher levels steadily improved. Despite the alcohol diet, which consumed me on a daily basis, I would not stop anything I was doing. I didn't know if I was making any friends during this period. I just knew I had a need — that need was to succeed.

In training with the Reserve Officers Training Corps, I also found more than one reason to push myself beyond acceptable limits. I spent three days a week doing road work and another two days were spent biking. All of this was done on top of all the time I spent in the gym. It was pure insanity at its best. I pushed myself not only to where I was tearing my body apart, but I was also delaying the healing process of an old injury I had suffered in Airborne school. I had to have orthoscopic surgery on my knee just to give me a fighting chance to stay in ROTC. After the surgery, it was a question mark as to whether I would be allowed to earn my commission. I worked endless hours with the athletic trainer at college to get back on the right track. Hot/warm treatments twice a day, in addition to a less rigorous workout until I got permission from the trainer to resume the insane abuse, I was putting on my body. Along with one of my fellow classmates, I was on the verge of making history at school in another year. I didn't want to shortchange myself out of all my hard work. A lot of tax dollars had been poured into my degree and into my professional development to become a commissioned officer. Honestly, some of it had gone into my habits of self-medicating myself. As much as I tried to fight it at that point, the bipolar illness was slowly, ever so slowly starting to erode away at my mental capabilities and beginning to surface.

However, right then, my symptoms were very subtle. My energies were challenged, and my obsessive-compulsive behavior, which caused me to do a lot of relatively reckless things, had been bridled. Unfortunately, I displayed a lot of channeled aggressive behavior towards my friends in the form of overly physical contact and a desire to prove I had overcome the physical setback with my knee and dominate in reckless activities.

I was ready for one final major hurdle as a prelude to being commissioned. I prepared for Reserve Officers Training Corps Advanced Camp at Fort Bragg, North Carolina, home of the 82nd Airborne. However, I couldn't be just your contemporary airborne cadet. I had to be a hero and drive down to North Carolina instead of flying down. Thinking ahead of myself, I thought I would have the use of my vehicle on the weekend, but to my chagrin my truck was locked up behind concertino wire for the duration of camp. The weekend prior to graduation I was allowed to take my truck out and make a quick snack run to Burger King, then have about 60 minutes' worth of liberty off the base. The night prior to having access to our vehicles, our platoon of cadets had a party at the local military canteen to celebrate our graduation. Once again like a fool I allowed my body to become saturated with alcohol, which very quickly dehydrated me. I staggered back to the barracks when, as luck would have it, I stumbled upon the platoon tactical officer, Capt. Hutchinson, who was just about the last person I wanted to be running into at that point. His job was to evaluate cadets to see if they were fit for active duty. At that juncture, even though I knew I was a very prolific writer and speaker, he liked the fact that I was very devoted to my duties, and clear and concise in my writing skills, but he didn't like seeing me abuse alcohol on the eve of graduation. As I looked into his eyes, I felt that whatever chance I had on getting a recommendation for active duty had been defeated by my own professional negligence.

In the six weeks of Advanced Camp, although Capt. Hutchinson and I had developed a mutual admiration for each other's wit and savvy, my skills as a soldier had something to be desired. Basic training could only teach a person so much about being a leader. There was not enough time for me to improve to the acceptable levels I desired, much less what Capt. Hutchinson wanted. My wit and intelligence had carried the day on many occasions and in all likelihood had kept me out of a combat arms branch, which would have gotten me or someone under my command killed.

I was not fully aware something was wrong with me as of then I just knew I had a conscience—if there was anything wrong with me, and I could go to any extreme to identify myself as being bipolar, I would have, but I was only a young man with a degree in History and soon to become a 2nd Lieutenant. If only I had known then what I know now, my life would have been more desirable.

The issue of marksmanship came up again. By then I was wondering if anybody other than me was following trends throughout my history on the range. At that point we were given a few rounds to practice with. I took my first shot. My scorer said, "Bolo." Then I threw a rock at the target, and the scorer said, "Hit." It was going to be one of those days. Forty rounds later I had hit the targets 28 times. I wasn't completely sure, but I think Capt. Hutchinson was starting to notice a pattern. Yet there was nothing concrete about my different types of behaviors as of right then. One thing that *did* begin to standout, however, was the fact I was experiencing mental exhaustion. My brain at some point seemed to be crying out for relaxation, which in wartime is a luxury you will not receive. My fellow classmates (platoon members) were trying to be as nice as possible concerning my poor sleeping habits, but I just couldn't hang in there at times. To be candid, I was ashamed of myself. For the first time since I had donned the uniform, I felt like I was openly abandoning my duty. We had adopted a tool from basic training called the Z-monster, which was nothing more than being slapped upside the head to keep me awake. Every time I was lax, I was punished with the Z-monster. After weeks of somebody slapping me upside the head, I was ready to fight for something that was beyond my control, but there was nothing I could do about it.

Fort Bragg was a true adventure. That was where I learned to become a true leader and to deal with the issues surrounding the bipolar illness for the next few years. I didn't know that one day the demon in me would be unleashed somewhere or somehow. I knew something was wrong, but I didn't know what. I just knew the current mission I was on was to evaluate me for active duty, which is what I got when I received my first "branch of choice" in the Army. It was time to be a hero. The true test of me being able to control the mental exhaustion associated with the bipolar illness was with the company's field training exercise. Even though I had performed as a leader and showed potential, I had failed at almost every aspect of my soldiering skills, due to my bipolar illness. Again, Capt. Hutchinson showed disdain and outright concern. Despite my vigor and energy, I knew I was about to be lectured on my lack in professional judgment. Oddly enough, the lecture did not come on the night when I most expected it, but on the last night of Advanced Camp after I had had a chance to rest and clear my head.

I shake my head as I type this. After all these years, the memories still have not faded. I recall the good captain looking at me and shaking his head with so much doubt in his expression that I could sense it. With a sigh, he just asked me point blank what my goals from Advanced Camp had been? I was firm in my reply. I would never quit being a hero, bipolar or not. "Sir," I said, "with all due respect and honesty, I would like active duty, but down deep I realize, after personally reviewing my own performance, I know you can't make that recommendation. If you can't make that recommendation, I would at least like to be given my branch of choice."

I had put the gentleman in a rather difficult position. Instinctively, I knew I was not going to get any of my choices. Why did I have to be so naïve at that point? Then for a reason that I didn't instinctively understand, he dimmed the lights in the tactical office because I was squinting excessively. He didn't say a word right then. He just politely dismissed me with my evaluation, which I wasn't so sure I wanted to read. However, it didn't turn out to be as negative as to what I thought it was going to be.

It said that he was impressed with my ability to write and communicate, but beyond that, he thought the only thing I would offer to active duty was leadership. Well, at least I was doing something right, I thought to myself.

My journey home from Ft. Bragg was completely uneventful, except for a downpour of rain which nearly put my truck in a ditch. I was quite reckless in my drive home. Sometimes I came close to revving my engine up to 85 miles per hour. I didn't realize that I hadn't checked the oil on my vehicle when I left Ft. Bragg, which could have been disastrous on the drive home. I was always the absent-minded person when it came to that. It would go on to cost me two blown engines on that truck at a later point in time due to my negligence, but at least Advanced Camp was over. It had been one learning experience I would never forget.

My senior year in college brought all kinds of chaos into my life from what I now perceive to have been caused by the bipolar illness. I did such insane things that year, all the way from off the road trucking to becoming an assistant pledge master for my fraternity, a position I kind of abused. Either that or I was sort of in an uncontrolled manic state at the time, which might have explained my uneven temperament.

My ability to pay attention to detail had really begun to plummet. While we had a positive break in the weather that spring, the Blue Mountain Battalion from Dickinson College, which included several other schools, had scheduled a field training exercise. One of the exercises for the weekend was a land navigation course. The day had gone extremely well for me until I set my compass down on a stump and walked away from it. Within seconds the tactical officer noticed I didn't have my compass and jumped on my case almost instantly. Another cadet and I were instructed to go searching for the compass. Mr. Dan Pagano, I apologize for dragging you two miles down that icy trail to compensate for my shortcomings. I was even more embarrassed when a freshman came jogging down the trail and told me the compass had been found. I maintained my silence until I got back to the dormitory that night. I had made a cardinal mistake and didn't know what had come over me that day.

The military was not the only place where I suffered

due to a lack of diligence. I was shocked by the mental mistakes I was making in school as well. The worst part was that these chronic mistakes were beginning to cost me financially and physically. To compound matters, I continued to drink. I felt like I was a clinical experiment with no guidance. I couldn't blame anybody but myself. Somehow, every morning I was hoping to get newfound relief, but it never came.

Despite the fact that it seemed as if none of my peers reached out to help me, I had a strong focus on my classes and my future career. My history classes kept me motivated, even though I marched forward without having recognized I was bipolar. My personal enjoyment in my degree kept me motivated with the willpower to succeed in my academics.

V.

A Complete Turn Around

The biggest day of my life, and probably the highlight of my academic career, came in the spring of 1989, when I graduated and took my Oath of Office. History had been made at the school for the first time since the college had invited the Reserve Officers Training Corps to play and active role in the development of student leadership. As far as the bipolar illness was concerned, I thought this was the end of it. However, my career as a professional soldier was about to spin out of control. The next 27 years of my life were about to create new challenges which I couldn't foresee. I can't begin to relay this experience to a point just for the pain and challenges I had to endure, but the purpose in writing this document has been to help individuals who have had to deal with bipolar illness, whether they are enduring it alone or with the help of the support groups that exist for them. I want others to see how much work it takes to help individuals with the bipolar illness to lead successful lives.

After graduation, my next stop before going to Germany was to complete the Adjutant Officer's Basic Course at Fort Harrison, Indiana. This was what I had trained for, and this was the reason why ROTC had invested in with a three-year scholarship in college. My leadership training was about to pay dividends. I had taken the summer off to help my father with his business and had come away from the business full of fire. My father and I worked well together, even though I was bipolar. I should have been content to stay there because I probably would have gotten treatment quicker, but I wanted to see the world one last time before committing to something for the rest of my life. I had orders in hand and was ready to excel to the best of my ability one more time. My report date to the schoolhouse at Ft. Harrison was Oct. 14, 1989. This would be my chance to prove I was worth the time the military had invested so heavily into me. Deep down, I knew I would not be denied this opportunity.

I am now sitting here smirking, because I am 53 years old at present and still think back to my glory years at Ft. Harrison. I keep on thinking I need to live up to those same expectations. Something tells me that I can reach down deep inside one more time and still do it. The fact is, I am not supervising military personnel anymore, plus I don't have enough hours in the day to drive myself to that prior level of expectation, even though I keep on thinking it should be so easy to do.

Anyway, when I arrived at Ft. Harrison, I was as giddy as a new schoolboy. My bipolar illness was not an issue for the short term anymore, even though I was acting as if it was. But I was still afraid of acting strange and not positive in a new environment.

My life always seemed to go a little bit better when I drank to take the edge off, and my first week at Fort Harrison was no exception to that fact. I started to drink again during that time period for what I thought was just being sociable and because things seemed to go more in my favor. As soon as stress built up and aggravated my condition, I didn't hesitate to go to the Officer's Club to release my aggravation. I could damn myself for the day I ever started drinking again, even though it felt like it was subduing my condition. I was just fooling myself to believe that. I was just laying the groundwork for a lot of things to go wrong in the future because I couldn't refrain from drinking. However, I had always been a wishful thinker, so at that moment I could think only of all the positive things which could have gone right in my life if I had never started drinking for an evil I didn't understand. I know I can't blame this whole situation on the military, because the Army was not the one holding the bottle for me and drinking with no regard for the consequences, but both parties in my case settled the score with one another and moved on. I moved on to enjoy some years of professional success, and the Army went on to win more wars without me. I am smiling at this point because now I have a chance to rebuild what I lost 12 years ago and to really feel good about life again.

Once again, I had set myself up to be the bolo King.

The king of all marksmen, who could not hit the broadside of a paper barn if you paid him to. My efforts quickly became a class project and not just an individual effort to qualify. New glasses, binoculars, throwing stones. Finally, out of desperation, the cadre members of my OBC class took me to a very isolated range. I was given 480 rounds of 5.56 mm ammunition. The command was given: "Lock and load one ten-round magazine, place your selector switch on semi, and prepare to defend your position." This was all too familiar. I couldn't see to save my life, so with almost five hundred rounds of ammunition, I was going to blow away my target board. (At this time nobody realized I was actually in the advanced stage of glaucoma.) Four hundred and eighty rounds later I had hit the target board 26 times, which was the minimum amount required by the United States Army. I still remember that whole affair like it was yesterday, even though I don't recall a single one of the names of the tactical officers who were with me then. There were approximately three and a half years left in my Army contract after that, and it was the last time I was ever going to qualify.

Not only did the entire Army not realize I was bipolar, but nobody realized I was suffering from glaucoma. Between those two illnesses, I could never get it together when it mattered the most. However, despite my ailments, I had something the Army wanted: leadership ability. It was hard to imagine that the Army was hard up for real leadership, but that was something I had plenty of.

I was ready to damn my soul on that particular issue, right then and there.

Finally, the day came when our orders were in, and yours truly was not going to Germany to become a part of a war-making PSC. Instead, I was rerouted to the nation of Belgium to serve as the community adjutant for the NATO/SHAPE Support Group. That place was its own mini hell within itself. They wanted me for my leadership, and if it hadn't been for my various illnesses, that was exactly what they would have gotten.

MONS, BELGIUM—Stage Right

During my first three weeks in Belgium, I was living in a military transient facility. It took me two whole nights to find a drinking hole three blocks away from the billets. I was called the Lion's Den. The place was my first introduction to Belgium beers and the Belgian culture. My first night out drinking, the beer literally knocked me on my ass so bad that I had to crawl my way back to the transient hotel. The next morning was my first physical training test with the company. I suffered to no end, but I was young and exuberant, so I pushed myself and did my best. Despite the punishment I endured, I was determined to make an impression on the local Belgian railroad workers the following night at the Lion's Den. I was incredibly determined to show these hoodlums what my sixteen-inch biceps could do in arm wrestling, especially with somebody else buying all the beer.

Every time I participated in an arm-wrestling contest that evening, I won with ease. Each time I won the loser had to buy me a beer. By the time the evening was out, I was seriously plastered, but I hadn't lost a single arm-wrestling contest that evening. As journeys to the Lion's Den carried me forward, I didn't lose one arm-wrestling contest in three weeks, no matter how excited I became every night. Overall, what a good experience it turned out to be! However, it also scared me because it seemed to be a continuation of the binge-drinking I had done every night in college. I was drunk every night then, and I really didn't understand why I was doing it. There was no enjoyment in it. I was trying to hide something—I just didn't know what. Deep down, I wanted to grow up, quit drinking and become a more appealing person. I could not even muster the courage to do the right thing from day to day. That scared me even more than the abusive drinking itself. I was in for an adventure that I wanted in the worst way, yet I *didn't* want it. The fear of the unknown was about to catch up with me and drive me to a whole new personal level I had never anticipated.

I was young and foolish. The bipolar illness was starting to rage inside of me like an unleashed demon, so I didn't realize the consequences of my actions. I didn't even understand what I had to do on my job yet. Representing someone with the power and authority of Thomas Eanes, Commander of the NATO/SHAPE Support Group was something that should not have been taken lightly. I represented the Commander of the Support Activity for the nation of Belgium. Like a very unwise lieutenant, without even thinking twice about it, I was jeopardizing Eanes' position with every beer I drank. Even though I was king of arm wrestling at the Lion's Den, impervious to pain and beyond defeat, I was jeopardizing my boss's reputation. This unacceptable behavior of mine went on for weeks, and sometimes it even carried over into the office. The rage inside of me made me feel like the Greek god Hercules. I really believed everyone, civilian or military, had to do as I commanded. The sense of power had gone to my head. However, my narcissism was about to be placed in checkmate by my Commander, and the demons which dwelled within me were about to be unleashed.

I was working on a line-of-duty investigation where a soldier had been killed in Norway. I was not treating the summary court investigation with any sense of urgency. My Commander walked back to my office to inquire about some efficiency reports and to ask what the delay in the summary court investigation was. I had no straightforward answers, so like a fool I exaggerated the first thoughts that came to my mind. My Commander knew I was talking trash; he raised his voice to the point where for the first time in my life I thought I was going to melt in my tracks. I feared the man from that day forward. The Hercules inside of me disappeared and was consumed by everything except respect. That was the first and only time I allowed myself to be embarrassed in front of my troops.

Some medical doctors have attributed bipolar behavior to being passive/aggressive; if that is true, this was the first time in my life I can honestly say I hated someone. The passive/ aggressive tendency in me just fueled disaster for the upcoming evening's events. I thought I had reached the point where the hounds of Hades had finally come for me, and it would take all my wit to avoid them.

That night at the Officer's Club there was to be a formal black-tie dinner for all the officers in the military community. By the time I arrived at the club I was already on edge. I tried making conversation with other company grade officers I worked with, but my thoughts were disjointed and tangential. I felt like I didn't fit in. I felt somewhat inferior at that point, which I used as an excuse to buy another beer and then another one to quickly follow suit. Each beer I drank fueled my anger and got my adrenaline pumping. I was ripped and ready to roar.

Finally, two of my fellow company grade officers saw the state I was in and quietly tried to keep me away from the bar. I saw their actions as threatening in nature; this made me feel more aggressive, which was a terrible attitude to have for that time of the evening. I was putting myself in danger without any realization of what I was doing. Then it had to happen.

The following is one memory I hate to relive, but for the sake of showing how devastating the bipolar illness is, I feel compelled to share it. I had just purchased a brand new 1990 Plymouth sports coupe from the local retail dealership and had not had it for more than a month. To make matters worse, I was experiencing some manic ups and downs at about that time. I had decided self-medication was the best thing for me at that point to help me tolerate the situation. I was a time bomb on a delayed fuse. Even though my friends were trying to help me, I needed to lose myself that night. My brain was on fire. I was cycling information very quickly. That, combined with the intensity of the alcohol, made me want to flee from the party instead of becoming a part of it.

My friends confronted me again and tried to get me to surrender my keys. By then my speech was slurred. I was flushed with anger and could not understand how or why I was going this to myself. My judgment was off base, and my anger was misdirected towards my friends in uniform. To this day I am still ashamed of my behavior in uniform that evening. I refused to listen to anybody's rational advice that night. I only wish I could have those ten minutes of drunken infamy back to do over. My imagination started running wild and kicked into high gear. I imagined I had to go to Brussels in the dead of night on a top-secret mission to deliver some encoded documents. My thoughts were definitely shooting off on a tangent. To make matters worse, I had not yet surrendered my keys to anyone, and I was determined to be a hero from that moment on.

Being the unfocused hero I was at this particular point, I jumped into my beautiful sports coupe, threw my briefcase in my backseat, and off I went to pursue my secret mission that I alone knew anything about or could justify to anyone. Ole Miss to Creativity I was.

This story is a tough one to share, but I'm going to anyway, because everyone who suffers from emotional duress needs to be aware of how razzled their behavior can be if they're not on the proper medication. Right then, the only medication I was on was alcohol. I was speeding onto the auto route going to Brussels and didn't hesitate to take my little sports coupe up to 85, maybe 90 miles an hour. To make matters worse, it was raining quite heavily. So, everything that could potentially go wrong that night was probably on the verge of going wrong and did. My car ruptured a tire. Within seconds I drove my car off the highway into a tree that was substantially bigger than my car. The only thought racing through my mind was that I was going to die. I could not think of anything else.

I had totally lost control of my car. I probably saved my life by letting go of the steering column and covering my head and face as I crashed into the tree. The tree cracked my chassis straight down the middle. I thought I had died. Then the explosion of the airbag brought me back to reality. I felt an incredible pain shoot up the right hemisphere of my head. That pain would end up haunting me for the next 20 years of my life. I crawled out of the wreckage of the car. For some reason I thought I had to bring my briefcase with me, so I just sat there beside the car, totally stunned, with my head between my knees.

What ran through my head was the thought that I had completely messed up. In my mind, my career was over. I had committed a DUI while in uniform in a foreign country. I was not fit to be a leader, much less take care of myself. I was utterly unfit for duty. If I had had any wit within me beforehand, I didn't know where it had gone. I wondered how I could have been so ignorant. I just sat there, shaking my head and ignoring the pain that shot through my brain. I was finished, and I knew it, but for some reason I thought it was necessary for me to go out as a fighting champion.

Within seconds, I heard sirens over the horizon. I thought, "Am I going to let them see me sweat?" I was still the Adjutant of the NATO/ SHAPE Support Group until Col. John T. Eanes said otherwise, which had not happened yet.

Despite my bravado, I thought at that point that I could do nothing right. But Lady Luck must have been looking upon me favorably at that point, because I had not been charged with anything.

I am shaking my head as I type this. I have never forgiven myself for being so naïve that night. All of this just because I didn't know how to cope with being bipolar or to deal responsibly with my mental health issues. I didn't know what the word *psychiatrist* meant, and there I was, sitting here damning myself for not paying closer attention in my psychology class instead of being hung over every night of the semester. If I had had a lick of sense, I might have been able to psycho-analyze myself long before the accident had ever occurred or long before I had ever gotten in the Army. Damn my soul for not thinking before I acted. I was fortunate to have survived that night, bipolar or not.

The hero of the evening was Lieutenant Kim Johnson. I don't think she realized the full impact of what she did for me that night. I was stunned and in shock, not really aware of anything. The only thing I knew I wanted to do was flee from the scene of the wreck. At that point I had no fight left in me anymore, and Kim was the only person I knew in the area. I would not listen to any of the medical personnel in the Emergency Room of the hospital where I had been taken by ambulance. The ER doctor tried to reason with me, but I was still hung over and well beyond the point of listening to him. I was obsessed with getting out of the hospital, because it appeared the only person who spoke English was the ER doctor himself.

My head was spinning. I was not aware of the severity of what the doctor was telling me. Apparently, I had a concussion, which it was nothing to mess around with. But I was the heroic adjutant and thought I could deal with anything. In my mind, I was impervious to harm because I had a security blanket. I was still in uniform and had Kim's phone number in my briefcase. I was very much hoping she would take it upon herself to come to my rescue that night. I knew I was asking a tremendous amount of my friend, and I have never thanked her properly for her heroic efforts that evening, because I felt I had to be so macho the entire time.

I just couldn't understand how I could have been so reckless. I was in my dress blues, yet I was drinking and driving. I didn't even know ~~when~~ what a breathalyzer was until that night. I really don't understand how I passed the test at all.

My confusion did not stop there. Instead, my irrational behavior continued on throughout the night. I finally called Kim at around 2 AM to tell her what had happened. The ER staff wanted to keep me at the hospital for the rest of the night for observation, but I had to be stubborn about it. The night had been nothing but a comedy of errors thus far, so I might as well keep on rolling while I was ahead of the ballgame, or so I thought. I was full of command decisions. As soon as Lieutenant Johnson showed up, I elected to leave the ER. The rage inside of me kept on building; I couldn't believe I had been so foolish.

I was a fool, and I knew it. My choice of words was undesirable to say the least. I am even hanging my head right now as I think about it. I somehow knew I was combatting a personal demon inside of me, but I could not convince anyone this was the case. I think it hurt more that I just couldn't bring myself to face the truth about the personal demon inside of me. When my friend Kim showed up and took me back to her place, she tried to help me calm my nerves. It was a hopeless task. It took hours before my temper began to subside.

Finally, she offered me a cup of tea, which calmed my nerves and slowly began to take effect. I was still very keyed up. I thought I had to be a superman one last time by returning to duty the next morning. I couldn't accept the fact I had screwed up so much. This was going to royally haunt my remaining time in uniform and cost me a promotion I had worked very hard to obtain. I can't fault the military for denying me my promotion. Honestly, I don't know who to blame for the mental anguish I had to endure right then. I was taking this adjutant thing way too seriously, and I was only defeating myself.

Somehow, I convinced Lieutenant Johnson to take me back to the headquarters building the following morning. We both had to be there for duty. She tried to persuade me not to go, but I snapped at her, and she backed away. She had been up the whole night trying to doctor me. If there was a true hero in this story, it was Kim. At that time, I don't know if she still considered me as her friend, because I wouldn't listen to her. If I had not been so bull-headed, my military career might have taken a turn for the better with Kim's help. She could have helped me become a first-rate officer with a flag grade career, even though I was bipolar.

While Kim shuttled me back to the Headquarters building, I began to realize how mortal I was. I had to confront the Commander about what had happened the previous evening. You'd think if I had had any common sense, I would have waited a day to rest up a little bit. No, not me.

Kim was still thinking of me right up to the end. She wanted to go into his office with me, but I would have none of it. This was not her ass-chewing to take; — it was mine. My career was ruined, but I was going to go down with my head held high, no matter how much pain I was in. The concussion pounded through my head that morning. I barely had the ability to maintain my focus on the Commander. If I had ever addressed Col. Eanes appropriately, it was that morning, even though I could barely focus on pronouncing my words correctly. He looked at me directly. His eyes burned into my soul as he sternly and directly said, "Lieutenant, you messed up royally."

I didn't know what to say. I was getting more depressed by the moment. Perhaps this was the start of the mood swing I didn't know about, along with everything else. Undoubtedly, the concussion had triggered manic-depressive behavior. No matter how hard I tried to fight the pain I was in, it was an uphill battle which I had no chance of winning. My day in purgatory was about to begin, and my eternal hell was about to take another step forward that afternoon.

The group had a five-mile run scheduled for that afternoon. I was about to discover what post-concussion pain was all about. My eyes were watering, and my voice was choking as I sounded off with the adjutant's call. I couldn't concentrate on anything as I attempted to do the adjutant's walk. The pounding in my head intensified more and more with each passing second as the words ricocheted in the right hemisphere of my brain. Somehow, I choked out my commands while my dear friend Kim looked on. She was almost in tears. Out of all the friends I have made in and out of the military, Kim has earned a place in my heart that is second to none. To this day I will never forget what Kim did for me that night. Because of using a little common sense, she somehow salvaged my military career for a few more years before I had to make a hard decision and leave the service myself. Kim helped me grow up into becoming a man sooner than expected. Through her mentoring I learned to take more serious responsibility for my actions.

The Group Commander showed no mercy on that particular run. I had a responsibility to the unit. Regardless of how much pain I was in, I was expected to fulfill my duties. The non-commissioned officer in charge realized I could barely hold the pace of the run. He tried to encourage me as the pace of the run quickened. Finally, the run was finished, and the Group Commander dismissed the formation.

However, my tail was still in trouble. The Company Commander was about to have a piece of me, no matter what I said. She came over to me with a look of anger, but empathy in her voice. She knew what had happened. Without sounding overly sympathetic, she proceeded to chew me out. I just looked at her. My tail was already thin from so many ass-chewings that day ~~already~~, that one more from a senior-ranking officer was not going to faze me. She closed out her remarks by saying, "Son, you are in the military now, so you had better damn well start acting like it."

Well, I could have said, "I just discovered I was bipolar last night," but I didn't know that for sure, and neither did anybody else. I had a hunch that my life was not going to be very fruitful from then on. I looked at her rather complacently and realized she was very serious.

"Damn my soul for getting myself into this position," I thought.

The post-concussion aching continued in the right hemisphere of my brain, causing pain that drove me to the local medical treatment facility at SHAPE (Supreme Headquarters Allied Powers Europe, Belgium). I knew the specialist in charge at the ER—Lisa. She could see almost instantaneously that I was gripped by pain of an unknown origin and maybe some other forces she had never encountered before. She whispered in my ear, trying to calm my fears, but I think that was beyond her beautiful voice that day. The doctor who was on duty was a full bird colonel who barely glanced over me. The only thing I recall is that he insulted my integrity by implying I was avoiding my military duty. My anger nearly exploded. This man clearly didn't understand that the right hemisphere of my brain was on fire. I had a profound fear of the unknown as to what might happen if things went catastrophic. I cried as I left the Emergency Room. Lisa followed me out in silence, sensing the pain I was in. I knew I had to somehow deal with this issue on a proactive basis in order to survive.

After the examination in the Emergency Room was finished, the Group Commander wanted me to handle troop-oriented details, in order to sharpen my basic leadership skills and give me a chance to catch up to other company-grade officers with similar types of duties. I was appointed the Executive Officer of the Headquarters Company. I thought a change of assigned duties would help me sharpen my leadership skills and decrease the amount of time I spent self-medicating. To some extent it did, but in the long run it did not. The concussion syndrome intensified, especially when the unit went to the local indoor range, and my glaucoma grew more intense when I tried to qualify by myself. I was never going to qualify at that point in time, unless an act of God interfered by throwing rocks at my targets. Between my headaches and my eyes, I prayed that somehow things would resolve themselves.

My pain was not meant to stop there, however. For some reason, the Headquarters Company Commander had decided to enter a team from our unit into the 21st TAACOM Military Stakes Competition. She picked me to be the officer in charge of the team. I just hung my head when I found out. I was wondering if the chain of command was trying to punish me for the mistakes, I had made six months before. What depressed me even more was that I didn't even realize at that point in my life what it was like to be a true leader. Right then I could only focus on my post-concussion pain. It was going to take every ounce of energy I could muster in order to pull this off.

The training started in the deep humidity of the summer. I had a chance to work with some of the finest soldiers stationed in the nation of Belgium, but I simply couldn't concentrate on putting myself in the role of the leader, due to the severity of the post-concussion pain I was in. So, until I learned better, I was just content to be one of the followers. However, when I was quickly trained to standard in military tactics and physical training, I took a back seat to none of my team members. I still couldn't qualify with my rifle, but I could assemble and disassemble a machine gun blindfolded in less than a minute, which was no small consolation for not being able to qualify in marksmanship.

Finally, it was time to travel to Germany for the competition. The most painful thing I can recall about the competition in Germany was the physical fitness test. When I saw the two-mile course, I knew it was going to test my physical limitations, but I had trained extremely hard and was determined to conquer the mountainside. My non-commissioned officer in charge challenged me to set the example on the spot. I thought to myself, "Why am I putting myself through so much agony?" However, it became an obsession for me to finish the run and prove I was worthy of being the leader. I do wish, though, I had taken a handful of aspirin before charging down the mountain so impulsively. I was either extremely competitive or borderline obsessive-compulsive. I finished the run in 10 minutes flat, which was a personal best for me, but with pain shooting out my eyes. I wondered why I was torturing myself that way.

People with the bipolar illness are sometimes noted to have abnormal sexual behavior. I was no exception to this. I thrived on the red-light districts outside of Brussels. This was a behavior pattern that not even my Commander expected. The first time I went to a red-light bar, I thought I was going for a drink with the boys. I was a country boy who was high on life and champagne, which led only to a desirable Belgian woman. This opened up a side of life I really didn't want to experience just then. My reputation was hanging in the balance, but at that point, I really didn't care. To my chagrin, this turned into a repetitive affair on a weekly basis.

Up to this point I had tried everything to deal with the insanity of my life and what it would take to turn my life around. The only thing that made sense was to drink insanely. I was extremely upset with myself about that decision and about the poor leader I was turning out to be.

I was confused about how things in my military career had gone astray so quickly. I was extremely hesitant to go back to old habits where I had found some peace of mind and had stimulated me, such as weightlifting, for fear of hurting myself due to poor concentration. It seemed as if others in my cohort like Kim really knew what was going on in their careers. Nobody had really taken time to analyze my problems, and since the medical opinions from the local military hospital had failed to turn up anything, everybody assumed there was nothing wrong. However, that was about to change quickly with the local Change of Command ceremony.

I had been in Belgium for approximately 10 months when the first change of command came about. By then my time in the office had taken a downward spiral. I was dating the most beautiful female enlisted service member I had ever known, which was the last thing my new Commanding Officer expected of his adjutant. Her strawberry-blonde hair was like no other woman's that I had been with in the past. Her lean and tight body was pressed hard to my muscular frame every morning. Yet from time to time I would still stray off into my foolish habits of previous months. Medically, I was going downhill rapidly. My post-concussion syndrome was running wild through the right hemisphere of my brain. The glaucoma in my eyes was burning, plus I was noted for being excessively generous in my personal monetary affairs.

I was really unsure about what I had gotten myself into, both professionally and personally.

For the past 10 months I had been aggressively harassed by a field-grade staff of lieutenant colonels, where there had been little fair play. I was just a young lad then; my efforts to help my boss were endless. He treated me as if he were a father figure to me when I proved my loyalty and commitment to him, despite my rocky start at the beginning of my military tour in Belgium. Between the future conflicts with Kuwait and Iraq and the ever-increasing irrational behavior I was exhibiting, I knew it was time for me to resign. My Commander thought I was making a mistake. He would not concur with my resignation, but I didn't have any more resilience at that time. However, until my resignation became official from the Department of Defense, the unit had a mission, and so did I.

The Colonel tasked my boss, the Director of Personnel and Community Activities (the DPCA), with developing a staffing project for managing the staff of the NATO/

SHAPE Support Group. I was the focal person for writing this document. When I received the assignment, I could barely snap a salute to the DPCA to acknowledge that I understood what was expected of me. I just rolled my eyes and left his office with pain ringing in my head.

I had never considered myself an alcoholic up to this point, but it was killing me not to have some sort of relief from the post-concussion pain. Whether it was the Officers' Club or the club at the airbase, I was there every night to drown my sorrows. The pain in my eyes consistently irritated me, which the enlisted soldiers who worked for me tried to understand. Those enlisted soldiers took me under their wing, because for the first time in ten months my leadership could not be counted on. One of my NCO's asked me why I let my boss treat me so poorly. I told her I was following orders, and until my new boss had more faith in my abilities, I would do my best to stand on my two feet. My boss was training me on the skills and arts of becoming a highly skilled AG officer, but I hated him for his ignorance about my medical problems, which I had tried to openly and directly explain to him.

There is a dangerous borderline between knowledge and ignorance, which was evident in this scenario. I had so much indirect anger at both the DPCA and the Group Commander that I knew I was going to fail the mission of writing the project, due to my pain and agony.

When I was able to put my pain aside, I thought professionally as a true gentleman. Taking on the challenge would be appropriate. However, I also had to deal with the glaucoma and the bipolar disorder, which no one knew I had. This affected my ability to make clear and concise decisions from that moment forward.

The end of the tenth month was the beginning of the end for me in Belgium. My internal demons were about to be unleashed. I was mentally exhausted from the previous night, and I was also ready to break down in tears, which was a characteristic of the bipolar illness. The drinking, adjusted workload, and lack of medical attention had driven me to the edge. Finally, I left my office and went down to the Company Commander's office, where I had a nervous breakdown. I took a chair into one of the back offices and cried my eyes out for two hours, hating life for what it had done to me.

VI.

Marching Forward to Germany

The Army's decision had already been made for me to go to Germany and maybe even the warfront, but the decision-makers had no idea of the injuries I had suffered and the mental abuse I had taken while being subservient to six field-grade officers. Tear after tear ran down my cheeks. I was embarrassed that a man of my position and stature was crying. I was going to Germany to a unit that was packed to deploy, and which was directly supporting units that were deploying. I was about to embark on a whole new journey that I hoped would find the cure for my illness. My thoughts were frozen every night, as I was praying for a solution to the problem that had plagued me for almost a year in Belgium.

Within 48 hours of receiving instructions from the Department of the Army, I received my marching orders to pack up and move to Germany on a no-cost move. I felt confident about the move, but I really didn't know what I was getting into. It would turn into an ordeal I never expected. It took me two weeks to get to Germany when I reported to my command. I thought I made a positive impression when I met my Commander for the first time except for the mild swings I was experiencing, but I was not intimidated by the challenges in front of me. My Commander had confidence in me. It was only the demon in me that would turn my life into complete chaos. I wish it had not been that way, but it was.

The mood swings energized me to the point of personal destruction. I was hurting myself. The intensity and drama of Desert Storm picked up, and so did I. My personal insanity would not keep me from accomplishing my mission and getting my promotion. However, the Commander thought I was going to burn out my troops and therefore pulled in my leash. My aggressiveness started to burn me out, and my mood swings were more apparent all the time. I had the most incredible urge to drive myself to a whole new level. I had a real-world mission. My reputation of being a first-rate AG officer was on the line, and I would not be denied. However, my negative behavior from Belgium caught up with me, and once again I was burning the candle at both ends. My misbehavior was becoming more apparent by the moment. Already I had begun to get the suspicion that various soldiers were complaining to the Commander about my personal life.

I thought I could prepare myself for any intellectual occasion, but my brain was not cycling information correctly. I had pulled the most stupendous tactical move an officer would ever pull. I thought I was slick enough to withdraw my weapon early for a field training exercise and no return it to the arms room at close of business that day. But the Commander caught me dead to rights, and I had no justification as to why there was an unsecured weapon in my office. I was finished, and I knew it. I made no excuse for my actions, but just shook my head in shame. The pressure was building up inside me. I felt the negativity growing, knowing that each new day would bring me closer to my demise in the Army. My negative energy was becoming incredibly apparent all the time. My Commander tried to counsel me about my poor performance on the unit's field training exercise, but I knew I was finished.

My careless behavior was taking place outside the office as well. As in Belgium, I also lacked a vehicle. The way I went about trying to get one could have gotten me relieved of duty if anyone had apprehended me in the process. Since I needed to go the local medical treatment facility one day, I took a Ranger pickup truck for a test drive. An hour and half later, I got back to the dealership and found out the dealership was ready to call the Military Police. I don't know why my Commander stepped in for me on that occasion, but he did. However, the pain in my head ricocheted to no end, and I knew it was only a matter of time until my days in Germany would come to an end. Why my Commander continually gave me the benefit of the doubt, I will never know. I knew I was in for a painful experience while I was in Germany; I just didn't know how bad this was going to be. Only then did I realize that the Commander was trying to become involved with my treatment for legitimate concerns.

I had to report back to the local hospital the following morning. This time my commanding officer was breathing down my neck to give me my marching instructions. I took the military bus there with my head pounding. I was not very confident that the local hospital could do anything for me.

This was a time of suffering I would recall for many days to come. I tried to sleep on the bus, but every little rattle made my head vibrate back and forth. I made it to the hospital without any more undue pain. I didn't know what to expect from the doctor's analysis or what to ask of him. By this time, I had given up all hope the pain in the right hemisphere of my brain would be going away. On the ride back to the company, I had so much pain from my concussion that I had to convince the bus driver to pull over, so I could find the nearest bush to crawl behind and vomit there. This was not how I envisioned my career in Germany was supposed to end.

Oddly enough, in my battered state the issue of weapons qualifications came up again. I didn't put up an argument anymore. The Commander knew I was a broken man, and he was going to put nails in my coffin. I had not qualified since I had been in Germany. Just to show the world what a lousy marksman I truly was, he was going to let one of our sister units evaluate me. I had no energy for such a task; my head rang out in pain at every possible moment.

I went to the range and found a place in the sun to take a nap until it was my turn to fire. At that point I had no desire to do anything else. I blew off 10 rounds, then went back to napping because the concussion rang so intensely in my head. I was in so much pain that I asked my Commander about the possibility of checking into the Landstuhl hospital a week early. Well, Commanders talk to Commanders, so I was thoroughly in the shit house when I got back to the company area that afternoon, but I was mentally exhausted, and really didn't care. I just wanted to hit the Officers' Club and drink it off. The Commander officer didn't really care from that point forward, either. He saw me as a pain in the neck, and he was looking for an easy way to get rid of me without actually understanding why. The day of reckoning was about to happen.

I walked down the hallway to the Commander's officer and requested permission to enter. Within seconds, I went into a manic-depressive mood swing and broke down in tears. My Commander must have been doing his homework up to that point, because the next thing I knew, I was on a three-day psychiatric stay in the Landstuhl Army Medical Facility. I stammered and stuttered, trying to explain what I was feeling to my Commander, but my efforts did not prevail. I had never asked to be this way. Even though I could see the anger in my boss's eyes, I could also see how much he understood.

I had done everything possible to help the unit survive Operation Golden Python which was our peacetime mission in Germany. I had elevated my performance to an all-time high, but eventually my efforts were in vain. My dreams of becoming a field grade officer were over. I didn't understand clinical treatment at that point. It just seemed as if things were going to roll in a negative direction for a long time to come. I have personal feelings about the whole thing, but right then I felt those feelings were irrelevant, because I probably didn't have the education or ability to apply myself to properly ascertain the situation. Perhaps my pain and suffering could have been better avoided if I had been more enlightened.

I loved my uniform, and I loved my personal mission in the Army, but at the same time I could not bear the onslaught of the pain my body and mind were being put through. When I was admitted to Landstuhl, I was given a psychiatric evaluation and started on a new medication called Tegretol. I didn't know what the medication was in a pharmaceutical sense, but I would soon see how it tempered my mood swings. My unit Commander was tasked with getting my personal effects together. The last time I saw him was when he brought my uniform to me hospital room and left me with a nice little compliment, saying I was messed up in the head. I thought that would be a rather rough memory to dwell on. In fact, it does surface from time to time. It makes me wonder if war actually has to be that cruel. I guess it must have been not exactly what I had anticipated.

It took an incredible effort to deal with the ups and downs of the bipolar illness while I was in Europe, plus all the negative attributes that are associated with the illness. I found myself constantly trapped by the bipolar illness. I am purely disgusted by some of the atrocious things I did. I longed to be number one among company grade AG officers, but my mind was trapped at every corner. I could not cope with stress as quickly as my peers. Even on a social level, my life had started to fall apart. The Commander was having a unit dinner on a fall evening. I wondered if I could compose myself and maintain my decorum throughout the ceremony. By the time dinner started, I had composed myself, only to be foolish enough to have a beer or two, which probably set me off again. I took a seat with one of my warrant officers, who took it upon himself to be my guardian angel for the evening. Thanks, Henry, for bailing me out of a tight one that night. I couldn't keep my big mouth shut. With one quick psychiatric outburst, I put all my pain on him that evening. I had suffered so much psychiatric damage from the past that I wasn't sure if I knew how to handle myself anymore. I had been punished to the uttermost extreme by my previous Commander.

My biggest problem is that I think I have to blame myself as much as anybody else for everything that has happened in the past. There are a lot of choice words I could think of right now, but I still remember I am a commissioned officer, and I need to maintain my decorum, especially now that I am stable, and people look to me for leadership more than anything.

I would be in the Landstuhl Hospital from three to five days with a preliminary diagnosis of post-concussion syndrome, which didn't tell me anything I didn't already know. I also knew that a lot of senior-ranking officers such as the one I had encountered at SHAPE, didn't know what it meant, either. My anger still haunts me to this day with the Emergency Room doctor the night of the accident. I made the rash judgment, he didn't. It took a year of suffering and misery to finally get the attention I needed. It was time I quit being a hero and do everything possible to get me life back. I was administered every psychiatric and psychological test in the book, yet for some reason I still felt like I was avoiding responsibility. I didn't understand what bipolar disorder was, and nobody was explaining what it was like to give me a fighting chance to overcome it. I knew I had a mental illness. After being in the hospital for approximately two or three days, I started to feel loopy. Finally, the decision was made to send me back to the states that very weekend. I was started on an antidepressant to get ready for the flight home. Negativity was an endless feeling at that time.

When I had a scheduled departure date out of Ramstein Air Force Base on a C-130, I was given Tegretol and an antidepressant to calm me before the flight.

My ability to focus was incomplete. I had a kind spirit in which I wanted to help everybody, even though I was completely incapable of doing so. Out of the corner of my eye I saw two airmen conversing about what I assumed was my medication. Out of pure curiosity I edged closer to them to try to listen in on their conversation. I could clearly hear what they were saying and felt I could help solve their problems. I don't think they understood what I was trying to do, and I also don't think they really cared. Between the two of them, they kindly escorted me back to my seat and made me very aware that I was not to leave my seat at any point. To make sure I understood their instructions, the flight physician gave me another Tegretol. I didn't wake up until the flight touched down at Dulles. When the rear door opened, the largest heat blast that had ever hit me did; — it was incredible. I had never been so happy to be on American soil. I gently kissed the ground I stopped on, then picked myself up like a real man and walked to the hospital shuttle, not knowing what I was getting myself into from then on. Previously, I had lived for every ounce of energy I had spent in winning my gold bar, but something told me I was on the verge of losing it. Down deep inside as I waited in the reception area, I knew this was it.

After 10 minutes of meandering in the reception lounge, my fellow veterans and I were taken to the Walter Reed Army Medical Center. However, the only thing that mattered to me right then was the incessant pounding in my head. It just wouldn't go away. I leaned my head forward against the seat in front of me and prayed for just one ounce of mercy, but I knew none would be forthcoming.

The shuttle bus unloaded at the hospital, and I was ushered into the psychiatric part of the hospital. When I approached the ward, I was going to be a part of, I asked what kind of unit I was being placed in. The nurse's reply was, "The post-concussion lock-down and observation ward." If they had had any other serious theories about what my diagnosis was, they would have been able to spend more time diagnosing the problem from there on out. But I had so much pain in my head right then that any means of analyzing my injury sounded great to me. There had been no direct diagnosis that I was bipolar at that point in time.

I Didn't Deserve This

My first night on the ward felt like a direct punishment. I sat in the hallway outside of my room and cried as I clenched my uniform. I tried to convince myself I was going back to active duty, but my tears were in vain. My tears were real and not as phony as the staff may have thought they were. I didn't even have to consult the medical staff to realize that my days of being a bull in a china shop were over, and I would not be returning to active duty.

My first true love in life was over. The crying continued. Quietly I hung my uniform in my closet and never found it again. I finally gave up on having any future career in the Army. I was asked time and time again to stay in the Army, which was like asking me to make an analytical decision without numbers. I felt like my intelligence was being insulted repeatedly, because I was constantly bombarded with negative thoughts. Medical staff members continually asked me if I wanted to go back on active duty. It was like trying to make a command decision without input or feedback from any staff members. In this particular case, I really didn't want to make a decision based on the input I was receiving. I thought the input was inadequate.

It was just one psychiatric test after another. I could hardly bear the insults to my intelligence. I felt I was beyond the stage of being constantly belittled. I cried myself to sleep every night, wondering why the staff couldn't do more to help me with the mental anguish I was experiencing. I could not even begin to fathom what my mental issues were just then, and I didn't even know then if I was bipolar or not. If I was bipolar, I was either in too much pain to understand or the medical staff was not very direct in explaining it to me. Every time I tried to ask about the issues that affected me, I felt like I was talking in vain. I was looking for a short and well-clarified answer, which never came. My soul was constantly under fire.

Every day became an ongoing battle with the medical staff. I couldn't deny the inevitable, even though I was very bullheaded. The consistent question from them was, would I like to return to active duty. Their close-minded mentality drove me to the edge and beyond. I tried to reason with them that a return to duty would jeopardize the lives of my troops, much less my own life, and would not be beneficial to anybody. If there had been an effort on their part to tell me what was wrong, they might have obtained the response they wanted, but that never happened. I was going to stand by my own judgment call, because I knew I could not change Army policy, no matter what. I was a leader, and nobody could change that, no matter how much it hurt. I just expected the psychiatric team at Walter Reed to do their job, and I would do my job as it was engrained in me to do. I was ready to concede to my psychiatrist if he could tell me what was wrong with me. Down deep I was hoping he would do this, because I felt a part of my manhood had disappeared without active duty, as I pointed out to the psychiatric team.

However, I was not going to jeopardize the lives of any US military personnel just to prove I could endure more pain than anyone else could. The team started to attack my character once again, and said I had a negative attitude towards active duty. But I knew I needed help, and the answers I needed were not being supplied to me, causing e undue mental anguish, which was not the right way for them to go about doing things.

I had reached the point where my anger was potentially starting to get the better of me, but I had to have an answer. In my professional estimation, I needed to get the correct response I deserved. As far back as I could recollect, I had been mentally ill and had gone through almost five years of suffering up to that point. Why I had been left to suffer for such a long time, I really didn't know. The pain I had endured along the way was going to make a true man out of me once and for all, supposedly.

Finally, after six months in a psychiatric ward at Walter Reed Hospital, I was discharged with a diagnosis of post-concussion syndrome. I was in pain every day.

At the end, my professional relationships with the medical staff were completely strained, my confidence was shattered, the pressure in my eyes was remarkable, and I felt that I had no future in the Army.

I was praying my father would offer me a job with his business. At least I knew I had some place to turn to, even if there was no real future for me there. I didn't hate the Army for my pain and suffering, because I was the one who had made the mistake in judgment, whether I was bipolar or not, but I didn't take enough time to reflect upon what had happened after the pain began to subside. I always had to be a hero, without realizing or analyzing what I was doing and how wrong my actions might have been. I had to realize I was only a lieutenant. We got paid to follow orders and generally speaking nothing else. I had failed to learn to think for myself by data collection and observation. What I thought was a well-rounded decision was hindered by my bipolar illness. I just couldn't seem to realize I had an illness at all times. However, a new story was about to emerge. It was time to go home and work for my father's trash hauling business.

When I went to work for my father, the first thing that was made clear to me was what would happen if I didn't keep up with the packer truck (garbage truck). I had been practically inactive for the six months while I had been hospitalized. I was determined I was going to stand on my own two feet and prove to my father and the rest of the world that I was ready to work.

The following day I had to see what I was truly made

of. My father and I had always worked well together. On the first day of working with him, between the two of us we picked up almost three hundred stops, even though my head was continually pounding. That morning the workday began at 4 a.m. which I thought was a little unreasonable. I got out of bed to the tune of a Rottweiler scratching on my bedroom door. Using my better discretion, I choked down a cup of coffee and followed my father out the door, where the packer truck was already fired up. It was good to be home, but not under those circumstances. Before I went out the door, our big Rottweiler growled at me for not remembering to rub her head that early in the morning. It was her daily ritual. I always let the rottie have her way, because she was an incredibly well-behaved angel. Even though I towered over her, I loved her enough to appeal to her better senses. She was very therapeutic in our evening hours, and I enjoyed our evening strolls. Adjusting to home life was more challenging than what I had anticipated. I found that riding the packer truck with my father was very exhilarating. It took about 10 minutes to warm up the truck every morning. Then we hit the road with all cylinders charging. I tried to help my father out to the best of my abilities, but sometimes the pain got the better of me. While I tried to remain focused on the task at hand, I silently cursed the memories of the pain which had been inflicted upon me. I just had to continually remind myself that what had happened to me was just as much my fault as anyone else's.

Probably *more* my fault than anyone else's, I have

to admit, because I pride myself on being a progressive thinker. I thought the answer lay within my family, but I was too bullheaded to listen to their experiences and that of other people. Perhaps the decision I had made to join the family business was not the right one. In all likelihood I was not going to be able to reverse my bull-headed decision. Until everything was done concerning the Army, I cursed myself under my breath and wondered if giving up the Army for the family business had been the right thing for me to do.

The only thing I can recall is that my life was spiraling out of control, and I can only blame myself for ignorant decision making. After reflecting upon this issue for over twenty-five years, I guess my assessment may have been right. I am the only person to fault for not being able to control my enlightened abilities. I didn't think before I acted, nor did I think through any of my actions. I quickly realized I was very fallible, plus I was the victim of my own success.

I have contacted only one of my former commanding officers and feel incredibly blessed that he has responded to my emails. He was quite the commander, and he still shows that he is the officer and the gentleman he was 28 years ago. It was easy to be immature back then and to tell all my previous commanders —where the hell were they when I was in a ton of pain — but I have matured beyond that. I am still an officer and a gentleman who would show them more respect than any other company grade would if the opportunity ever presented itself.

Getting back to the home front, I think once again

that working for my father's business was the wrong decision for me. My problem was that I was Mommy's little boy. I needed to find a place to hang my hat and sleep off the lingering pain of the concussion; there was no better place than home. With some reluctance I grew into the tasks and directions my father's business was heading in. Along with doing the curb-side recycling, they had a small commercial recycling service which my father ran for campgrounds and amusement parks. He ran a fleet of light trucks through campgrounds and parks twice a week. It was a nice little windfall profit for me, since I was allowed to pocket over $2,000 in recycled materials that summer.

The day actually came when my father trusted me with part of his business. He agreed to let me do the recycling run around Lancaster City by myself. On one given day when I was coming back out of the city, my impulsive behavior would lead from one bad decision to the next. One afternoon, when I was doing about 10 miles per hour over the speed limit, I thought I could beat a red light. This was only one of the erratic things I did within a short span of time that afternoon. Without hesitation, I entered the intersection when a white Cadillac pulled out in front of my truck. Needless to say, he had the right of way. I braked into the rear panel of the car. This was nothing but pure disaster for me. The driver and the passenger were an older couple. I knew right away I was in trouble. The accident was in the middle of the intersection. I wanted to walk over to the couple and say I was sorry for acting before thinking;

I wanted to explain that I was bipolar and hadn't taken my medication that morning. That wouldn't have been very bright of me. I was glad I had a little common sense left at that point.

Like a little boy wanting to go to a candy shop, I hitched a ride to the nearest dealership, which was repairing my truck and started to walk around, looking for my next truck. My immaturity would benefit the dealer that day because he recognized a new sucker had just stepped onto his lot and was going to be fleeced for a lot of money. He approached me and asked me how he could help me. I told him I wanted a beast with power. He showed me even more than I anticipated. There before my eyes was a big, gray, powerful F-250, three-quarter-ton pickup, with a red pinstripe. The truck was a diesel, and it was mine to be had. I fell in love with the truck from the first minute I revved the engine. I called my banker (my mom) and asked her to empty out my bank account and bring the money to the dealership where I was making a deal on the truck. I had become obsessed with the truck; I was going to have it, no matter what—the bipolar side of me said so.

However, having what was in my eyes the most awesome truck made it a total waste of money for my father's company. Unfortunately, this experience was going to let me learn the hard way about being obsessive/compulsive. This would be my father's punishment for me acting so spontaneously. I was about to regret giving up the $2,000 dollars I had used as a down payment on this beautiful beast. Initially, I figured I could get a high rate of return on my personal investment into the truck. My dream truck was about to be shattered by my driving incredibly recklessly in a snowstorm.

I was driving down a small county road that was piled high with the deepest of drifts. I was being overzealous and exhibited a ton of risk by taking my new truck out that day. I was driving very aggressively down a side road to pick up recycling when I saw a semi-trailer parked along the roadside. I began to panic. I couldn't pull over along the side of the road due to the height of the snowdrifts. I tried to hit the brakes. The only result was a skidding motion and a sick feeling as the cab of my beautiful Ford truck was about to be dashed into oblivion. I ducked very quickly, thus avoiding a lot of unnecessary bodily injury. I ducked just in time to keep the door from the semi-trailer from being smashed through the cab of my truck into my face. When nearby factory workers heard the wreck, they ran out and pulled me out of my demolished truck, then took me inside the factory. I was barely conscious. The confusion and chaos that would put me into a hypomanic state was not apparent to anybody but me. I had been incited to new heights of hypomania when I had felt like Superman driving down the highway. Now as I heard the sirens coming down the road, I began to relax and realized I was hurt more than I would eventually imagine.

As the cold set in, I felt myself slipping into shock. The paramedic team came into the factory and got me somewhat under control. They quickly got me focused and loaded onto the ambulance. My condition only seemed to worsen inside of the ambulance. The team encouraged me to maintain my alertness. I didn't know if the medical team was aware of the fact that I was bipolar or of the highs and lows associated with the medical inducement of shock and what I was going through. What really seemed to help is that the paramedics bandaged up the wounds cause by the glass shards from the shattered windshield of my totaled truck. By the time the ambulance reached the hospital, my parents were waiting there. I was released from the hospital after a short stay, but the damage to my psyche had already been done.

VIII.

The Horror Continues

At this point, my thoughts were in a smog, no matter what I was thinking. I had no self-identity. I didn't know whether I was a hick or a punk fan of classic rock. I would listen to my stereo all the time to soothe my nerves, but the increased volume merely drove me to a whole new madness. If I didn't stop, I was on a one-way trip to a lockdown ward, but I didn't stop. I continued to jive. It was an endless madness driving me crazy. Band music from the eighties kept me going at an insane pace. Eventually, I was able to get some rational control of myself when I realized I needed some real help.

I remembered I had pseudo-fallen in love with a psychiatric nurse. My heart pained for her at such a high level just then. The J. Geils Band music continued to ricochet through my thoughts as each hour of the day passed. Finally, I openly admitted to myself that I needed help.; I wrote a very long letter to my medical treatment team. It was garbled and very poorly written.

It was not a suicide note, but it got me the attention I needed.

This episode at home was a complete downside in mental behavior which led to a rapid change in my life. I wanted to make a positive change in my life by going out and buying a car. I had the money, but there was two feet of snow on the ground. Still I was determined and foolish.

It was evident that I had become obsessed with driving. I threw on a pair of jeans and tennis shoes without any socks, then flew out of the house in the dead of winter with my mind in a whirl, ready to jog down the highway to the beat of the band and then to the car dealership to buy a car, which did get me into a lockdown ward, thanks to my family.

On that ward, I was under constant observation by doctors and RNs. I needed to refocus on myself and society. But the only thing going through my mind was the insanity of the whole situation. My brain was wracked with incredible tension, telling me to bolt out of the hospital any possible way, yet somehow, I had discipline enough to do the proper thing. I wanted the pain in my brain to subside. I wanted everything to return to normal, no matter what it took. I wanted to regain peace of mind, but I knew all my efforts would be in vain if I didn't somehow cooperate with my medical staff. The Lebanon Veteran's Area Medical Center (VAMC) has probably been the most influential hospital I have been to where I have had a positive experience in dealing with them. The staff told me to relax and let them take the lead; then everything would be okay.

But for some reason I had to be a hero unto myself and continued to fight my mental illness. I was trying to obtain normalcy on my own terms—something I knew I could be completely comfortable with.

I finally came to the conclusion that I could not conquer the bipolar illness on my own; I would need professional help in dealing with it. I just wanted the day to come in which I would attain normalcy once and for all.

It appeared that the most important test for me to take was a critical thinking test. I had no idea what critical thinking would do for me, but I was anxious to find out. I wanted to know how much it would enrich me and end the immense pain I had been feeling. I wanted to see how my life and intelligence could be molded with the help of these high-class professionals. I wondered if they could help me with both short- and long-term goals while I was in the hospital. I assumed they would be acting in my best interest, so I responded accordingly.

Twenty-five years after that particular hospitalization, I realized that the test-taking and skills I gained from the efforts of my medical treatment team helped me grow as an individual, as well as manage the bipolar condition. To this day, I don't recall the exact wording of the critical-thinking tests, but it is as if the thought patterns of the tests are now instinctive and almost reflexive to me.

At this point, I was in a very troubled state of mind.

My mind was moving at a hundred miles a minute. I had been asked to read a trilogy by Dr. Kay Jamison, who had been diagnosed with the bipolar disorder. She related her problems to the rest of the world so clearly and concisely. I myself was in a troubled state of mind. All of my attempts to analyze myself were in vain. I understood what my medical team was trying to do, but it was a different and unique experience. I tried to relate my troubles to those of great minds such as Dr. Kay Jamison's. She is one of the greatest bipolar minds that has ever entered the professional community.

I started thinking that my medical treatment team was trying to make parallels between myself and her, but I will never know that for sure until I complete my PhD.

I was completely fascinated by how my medical treatment team helped me grow as an individual and improved my ability to manage my bipolar condition.

Finally, I was released from the hospital and allowed to return home. I continued working for my father for about six more months after that without wrecking any more trucks. Then I got my call from the VA to go back to school. I thought this was my break to become a teacher. But who was I kidding? In reality, I was going back to school to get a real degree in the eyes of the VA and to keep myself employed in the future.

It took me three years part time to complete my degree. I thought I had met a very special woman, but it never worked out. The most important thing is that my education *did*. I completed my second bachelor's degree and started my MBA. I was accepted to five out of the seven schools I applied to. My number one choice was LaSalle University, which I made plans to attend. I had to study for the GMATs, which I thought would be relatively easy to take. I felt my excessive studying would easily put me over the top. Actually, I did end up passing the GMATs with flying colors.

When I first started school at LaSalle University in September 1997, I was determined to complete my MBA degree. This was something that neither the VA nor any academic official thought I would ever be able to complete. I was working as an Inside Sales Account Manager in New Holland, PA at the time, and I was not having any problems with my medication or with my apparent illness. For the most part, both school and the job were going very well.

Unfortunately, that was not going to last forever. I was unable to maintain a high-quality job performance without having problems with the bipolar illness, which led to problems with my co-workers and managers. My trail of tears never seemed to end. Things just kept on progressing downhill in both my academic and professional lives until eventually I got laid off from my professional job, after working there for approximately 10 months. I refused to cut myself any slack at that point. I collected six months of unemployment. Actually, I should have checked back into the VA to get myself straightened out. Instead, I relied entirely upon my own initiatives and struck out for Philadelphia to try to gain employment as quickly as possible. This period of being without a job was exactly the break I needed to improve my grades.

Well, I succeeded in improving my grades and networking for a job for the short term, but at the price of long-term stability. In all likelihood I probably needed to see my psychiatrist at that point, which was something that never happened. Let's just say that other people interfered, plus I had a knack for letting them do so.

So, my journey continued down to Norwood Coated Products in Malvern, PA, where I became their cost accountant. I also continued with my voyage in my studies. I'm shaking my head at this point, because I wasn't stable, and things did not go well for me from the moment I walked in the door at Malvern. My employment there lasted for only three months, due to my instability. What I tried to do to keep myself stable in my personal and academic lives, I resorted to drinking again. That was not what my employer wanted. Within 89 days I had become unemployed again. With that I put in a phone call for help to the Lebanon VAMC. My life was upside down, and I was really confused, because I was off my medications. I still reflect on how irresponsible I was for allowing other people to manipulate my life concerning medication. This really affected me negatively. I don't think those individuals really gave a damn about what was happening to me.

Without meaning to overly reflect upon what happened to me at that period in my life, let's just say I spent six weeks in the hospital until I was balanced again. Then I went to live in a halfway house for another six months. The house I lived in belonged to a PA state representative who was quite the character, but he gave me a chance to chill out for six months and become level again. Thanks, Tom!

IX.

One More Chance

The most awesome thing that happened while I was in school was that I also managed to finish my MBA, this time at Lebanon Valley College, while I was living at the halfway house. At LVC, I didn't have any problem applying myself to the field of higher education once more. Locally, I thought I had the job I wanted. Unfortunately, the job didn't work out like I was hoping it would. In 2001, I kept on cruising to try to get a job in education as a substitute teacher. My efforts eventually paid off. I wanted to give education one more try, to see if I had what it took to become a Secondary Ed teacher. I figured I would go to school at night and work as a tax preparer/sub teacher during the day. This is where things became complex; I have always been good at making things complex. I needed my jobs to support myself and pay for school to better myself, but I came up short. After two years of part-time schooling, a 2.8 GPA was not good enough to make me a teacher. School had sharpened my skills as a student, but it hadn't done anything for me as a teacher. Oddly, the 2.8 GPA was a warm-up for big and beautiful things to come, beginning in 2004 and 2005, when I would start my PhD in Organizational Leadership and be able to work as an adjunct professor at Rowan State University in Glassboro, NJ. I was on my A game, and I loved it. I was also working as a tax accountant for a gentleman in Harrisburg.

This was the most incredible intellectual experience, that is, until October 2007. I could not have picked a worse day for myself. One simple mistake made during that month was about to rock my world for over seven years, and I would hate every moment of it. I had thought I was on my way to brilliant and beautiful things in my life, but somehow, I was to be denied.

My intelligence and good memory are things I always used to take for granted, even with the bipolar illness. However, in 2007 certain events have really made me think whether I should continue to walk down this particular path or not.

On the other hand, writing this book was made so much easier on the day I spent conversing with a most intelligent woman, whom I needed to reach out to and in whom I could be fulfilled. She took my greatest gift and inspired me to write this manuscript, despite the animosity I had towards the psychiatric ward for overlooking what had happened to me over seven years previously. This woman taught me to reach out and share again, in order to make others realize what it was like to suffer from a puzzling and debilitating illness and how tough it can be to weather the storm caused by such an illness as viral encephalitis.

Viral encephalitis is an inflammation of the brain caused by a virus. Some viral diseases, such as measles and rubella, can cause an inflammation of the brain. Other micro-organisms are also capable of triggering this illness through bacteria and fungi, which can be transmitted by parasites and mosquitoes. In my case, my medical treatment team has thought my own bout with the disease came from a mosquito, but the jury is still out on that one.

Once the virus is inside the blood, it migrates to the brain and may cause traumatic brain syndrome. The brain notices the invasion of the virus and mounts a defense to the immune system, causing the brain to swell. Typical symptoms of the viral encephalitis are created by the coordination of infection and immune activity. As recovery occurs, the individual may need long-term support and therapy.

This kind of thing is why I shake my head and wonder why I go through the misery I do. Is it just because I am bipolar, or is it because I tell lame jokes? I wonder if normal people have these issues as well. I would be very much surprised if they did, considering I have to go to therapy twice a week at the Hersey Medical Center for cognitive retraining.

Some days I truly wonder why things happened to me. It was October of 2007. I was an adjunct professor of accounting at Rowan State University in Glassboro, NJ. I was teaching Intermediate Accounting, which was quite a challenge, but I lived for it and hoped my students did as well after class. I had to stop at a three-way intersection by a body of swamp water when I was rear-ended by an SUV with an iron grill plate on the front end. Like a hero, I didn't call 911. Armed with my insurance information, I got out of my car near the body of swamp water and compared insurance information with the other driver. I also wanted to make sure he was okay. Up to that point in time, I felt like a million dollars. I was so incredibly naïve that I didn't even know what viral encephalitis was.

I struggled with class that night. The easiest answers to student's questions seemed to elude me. I knew I was better than this, but I couldn't seem to function at the expected level that was demanded of a professor of accounting. I didn't feel abnormal just then, even though my question and answer session had been slightly off base. I was just not measuring up to the standards of my students that evening. Perhaps I might have been stressed about the damage to my car and the upcoming insurance issues. I took it upon myself to dismiss my class early and headed back to Pennsylvania, only to wake up in a semi-conscious state in the Emergency Room of the Lebanon VAMC four days later. (Only certain relatives knew the complete truth about what happened during that period. I have asked them not to share the truth with me or anyone else at this POINT. I'm not ready yet to handle the whole truth about what happened in those 4 days.)

ANALYSIS

"The patient is a forty-year-old white male with a past medical history significant for bipolar mood disorder, seizure disorder, and PTSD. He was brought into the ER by his mother after being found in his house in an altered mental status, unable to express himself. He also teaches at a local university. Prior to this recent episode, he apparently had a very high level of functioning and was living independently. Unfortunately, given his current mental status, agitation, and inability to speak, we cannot obtain a good history. He is currently in an altered mental state and cannot speak, although he is able to follow simple commands.

I heard a voice. It was the voice of an angel, trying to tell me to relax. Then the torture came. Needle after needle ripped into my body; I was ready to scream out in agony. "Please help me," I thought. I could not even express my thoughts correctly just then. I heard her soothing voice again, but it meant nothing to me then because my vision was so clouded by anger. I had not even known what was happening to me at that point because I had no clear understanding of where I was. Hallucinations were a reality then, even though they were only in my mind, telling me this world was not for real. I had no recollection of where I was or how I had gotten there. I wanted to scream at the top of my lungs, but I gagged on something in my throat. Something was keeping me from speaking, and I was also sobbing in pain. I had a distorted and confused feeling as my body was peppered with needles AND IVS. Somehow, despite this pained feeling, I was able to drift off and get moments of sleep. Then the nightmares and delusions set in, at which point I became my own worst enemy for a period of almost three weeks.

So, there I was, trapped in the pit of my own mind, searching for peace and tranquility, yet somehow knowing I would never have it if I had to go through this random torture to prove I was the Master of the Game one more time. I didn't know if it was worth enduring. If I had had to give up on life at that split second, I think it was a commitment I would have made without hesitation. But somehow, deep down I knew I would not deny myself, and I would always strive to complete myself. What else could be thrown at me other than the complete darkness I was facing at that moment? Despite the overwhelming pain and sadness which wracked my body, I still believed I was better intellectually, morally, and insightfully for being able to endure the unforgivable burden that was being placed on my mind.

Then out of nowhere it hit me. The hallucinations had started when I thought my life was taking a turn for the better, and my system went into complete shock. Somehow, I awoke in a dream-like state at a state facility in Georgia. I had driven a rather old pick-up truck down there with the intent of selling lithium at street value, except that lithium really doesn't have a street value. Since I was bipolar, nobody would buy lithium from me. It was a loser's dream. A constable arrested me on a street corner, with my jacket full of lithium, because he thought I was going to overdose on it. While at the intake facility at the state hospital, I didn't know if I was in Lebanon or Georgia. Talk about easy confusion.

During this nightmarish reverie, my thoughts stopped for a second. I thought I heard a voice that meant something to me. I didn't recognize it right away. My thoughts froze, but my memory finally gave way. It was my mother calling out for me to wake up, but I couldn't respond. My mind was the only thing that could respond, whether for better or worse. However, my body was dead to the world. Even my breathing seemed extremely irregular. She cried out for me to please wake up, but I did not respond, no matter how many times I was prodded. I had no energy or emotion to react in even the most basic ways. I was in a void, an endless gap that didn't allow any interaction between myself and anybody else. I still felt the restraints digging into my flesh, holding me down. I didn't want to do anything to aggravate all the IV's that were burrowing into my skin. Then there were other voices, but outside of my mother's they were all blacked out. I thought I recognized one doctor's voice, but with all the pain I was in right then, it didn't really matter. If I had recognized the doctor's voice, I just would have screamed at him, wanting justification as to why all this was happening to me. I didn't care if they were saving my life at that point. It felt like pure and bloody torture.

There had to be a point where the insanity would stop and I would wake up and face the soothing, refreshing air of the world again. I sensed I would probably be impaired, but how greatly I didn't know. I was just hoping to have my old life back again. I highly doubted if that was going to be possible, but I was not going to give up without a fight. My goal was to be restored to a "premorbid" (or prior) level of functioning. I was willing to go the extra mile for any reason my medical treatment team said I needed to, in order to regain full mental functioning once again. I have since learned this is possible. While I need to be assertive in this whole process, I also need to be patient.

The hours turned into days and my thoughts became an endless torment. I heard laughter in the vicinity, thus torturing my senses. Apparently, somebody was enjoying life, but I wasn't. The only thing I can recall to this day through my mental haze was that the Philadelphia Phillies were in the World Series. The only logical thing I could follow and focus on was the cheering of the fans. I felt kind of humiliated because I couldn't become involved in the process. My body was just wasting away in tubes whose purpose I didn't understand, other than to cause me pain.

I became determined that my miserable existence would end one way or another, so I had the hallucination that in my weakened condition I was able to stand up under my own power on my own two feet. What a dreamer I was. I imagined the floor nurse was going to my room at that particular moment and was stunned that I was on my feet. (I was really bold while being so heavily medicated.) Anyway, for being very imaginative,

I got a really incredible sponge bath. At least I felt alive for the short term.

To make a long story short(er), reality bit me in the tail when I didn't wake up that day, and I realized I hadn't gotten a sponge bath. Then the day came when I actually did wake up. I didn't have a clue as to what was going on around me. I was shocked by my surroundings. I felt helpless. It is incredible what your imagination can do to you when your middle name is pain.

The nurses chose their words carefully as they tried to console me. I had beat death again. There is no feeling that can compare to that—when you have more faith in God than the devil can take away from you. I had lost complete track of time, whether it be morning or evening, and I had no idea how long I had been in the hospital. I didn't even know what hospital I was in.

Then she came in. A female doctor with long blonde hair and blue eyes walked into my room. I didn't say a word at first, probably because I couldn't. Anyway, she took a seat next to me and proceeded to tell me about the past couple of weeks, and about how they had almost lost me. Like this was something I really needed to hear, but she was simply telling me how it was. She also filled me in on other things, such as the fact that I was at the Lebanon VAMC with a viral infection on my brain. This was the part where I rolled my eyes and wondered who was teaching classes. I guess the hospital had forgotten I was a professor, and professors just don't check into hospitals with brain infections. This was getting better all the time. I wondered how this doctor would react if she heard my side of the story. If I could have talked, I probably would have not known what to say, anyway.

After all that had happened, I felt like telling the world that I was awake now, even though I was only somewhat aware of what was going on. However, I don't think anyone would have listened to me up to this point. To my surprise, my whole family entered at that moment, except for my father. I couldn't even speak just then. The only thing I could do at that moment was suck on ice cubes as I slowly rehydrated my body. All my siblings grinned at me and said, "Welcome back." Ironically, I didn't even know I had been gone. I can't remember if my mother was in tears then or not, but I had never seen her so happy to see me awake. My brother, TC, a Marine, told me to make up my mind about what I was going to do, so he could go back to Iraq and win the war once and for all. Then there was my baby brother Joe. I don't exactly remember his facial expressions, but this was one of the few times he ever gave me a hug. Then there was my little sister, who had flown in from California, where she was studying to be a nurse. I had tears in my eyes right then, wondering what had happened to me to put so much emotional duress on my family. My cognition was not working in my favor, but I was hoping it was only a matter of time until I regained it in full measure. I spent hours with my family that day, until my doctors reassured me, I was going to be able to move forward with the assistance of my medical treatment team. Then we all parted ways. I feebly waved to my family, hoping to reunite with them on a more positive note in the future.

My medical treatment team informed me that I was suffering from a viral infection of the brain, which kicked me where it really counted. I was used to making a professional living with my intellect and my memory; now I was on the verge of losing full functioning in those areas. The thought of losing all my cognitive skills was very intimidating, after I had worked so hard at establishing a career in accounting and teaching over the previous 10 years. I didn't think this was a loss I was equipped to handle. Those had been 10 years of incredibly hard work. Now I had practically lost the cumulative effect of four college degrees. I wondered if I could rise to the occasion and perform at the level of excellence once again. My gut feeling to myself was that I would not be denied. I would keep my rehabilitation moving forward with the highest degree of integrity and efficiency.

Despite my setback at Rowan State, I could not find an excuse to give up on my teaching career as of that point in time. I was determined to succeed, no matter what the cost.

However, I quickly discovered I had to be more patient with myself until I was able to regain more control of my life with some degree of forward momentum. My situation with my wrecked car was a legal nightmare, and I had not been medically or legally cleared to drive yet. However, I was very determined to keep on pressing the issue until it was resolved.

To make matters worse, I hadn't seen my house in several months and was really unsure how far behind I was on my mortgage payments. Only my mortgage banker knew the answer to that question. After I received the first fore-closure notice, my financial relations were too strained for me to care. Life was nothing but an uphill battle from that moment forward. Worse yet, I was extremely desperate for a job.

It was springtime, and my first order of business was not to grovel in my own self-pity for a change, but to seize the bull by the horns and decide what I was going to do with the rest of my life. Teaching it was, but where? Realistically, I was damaged goods, and I didn't know if I could hope for a college or a university to even give me a fair shake at that point in my career. I set my sights on Stryker University as my next goal to fulfilling my teaching destiny. In the fall of 2008, I was hired as an adjunct professor of Accounting.; t To my dismay, my medications didn't quite get the job done. By the spring of 2009, I had been compelled to resign, due to a student complaint that I had started to show an outbreak of the bipolar illness once again. The student claimed I had locked myself in a classroom and was talking to myself. When I was confronted by my boss, I simply offered my resignation to avoid embarrassment from the school. This was the low point of my teaching career.

By this time, it was the spring of 2009. One would think that for the short term I would have had enough of the Good Samaritan Hospital and the Lebanon VAMC for a little while, but for some reason this was not to be the case. It was the Spring Arts Weekend at Lebanon Valley College. For some idiotic reason, I was asked to play in a softball game between the Knights of the Valley and KALO. As a Knight, I had never been asked to play in any other softball game during my undergraduate years, and I will freely admit I am the world's worst softball player, but like a hero I agreed to play.

I was at the bottom of the batting order. Luckily, I got a hit. The bench for the Knights went nuts. Like the true base runner that I was, I nearly make it to first base, but I tripped just shy of the base, dislocating three fingers on my right hand. I am sure my fraternity brother was merely trying to be a Good Samaritan when he took me to Good Samaritan Hospital instead of the Lebanon VAMC, which left me with a surgery bill of $6,200 dollars. This not only shocked my system, but it left my checkbook stunned for the next year.

X.

The Final Countdown

From that moment forward, I must have been in a state of grandiosity. I was convinced I could live a dream, so I started company called Trash Commanders, with the intent of recycling scrap retail tires. It was an excellent idea on paper, except that I let two people influence me as to the way they wanted me to conduct my business. This was a major tactical error on my part. By the time I fixed my mistake of listening to the wrong people, it probably cost me the whole business, which took the wind right out of my sails. Why I didn't stick to my own instincts is beyond me. That was the biggest business mistake I had ever made.

I made bad decisions based on all kinds of unfamiliar input. Being hypomanic at the time didn't help my situation, either. Using unfamiliar management tools, I was making incredibly poor judgment calls. By the time I realized what I was doing, it was too late to correct the whole system. When I tried to, it proved to be a costly mistake.

My personal spending habits went wild. I was consumed with buying things I didn't need, just to say I had them. I wanted to be the Jones plus one and a half. I would go out and buy a truck, just to have a different truck for every occasion, such as snowplowing and construction materials disposal, as well as two one-ton trucks for tire disposal. My total personal debt on four trucks came to approximately $59,000; then the price of fuel went through the ceiling, because two of the trucks were diesels. For almost a year, I was driving four incredibly beautiful trucks financed by credit cards. I didn't stop at that, either. Between fuel expenses and miscellaneous expenses, I spent over $80,000 on credit cards. I was quite the lavish spender on fine restaurants, without being afraid to eat the finest steaks on the menu. I was living the good life, with no clear thought that I was headed down the dark path towards destruction. The whole scenario was step one on the road to bankruptcy.

Secondly, I had no idea what was going wrong with me medically. I was experiencing euphoria at every corner. Nobody really knew what to do with me or cared to help me at that point, because everything seemed to be so extreme. I exhibited tangential and erratic thinking, plus I was creating a bigger financial and operational mess than I knew what to do with.

There were a couple of people who really went out of their way to help me get my life reoriented. The first was my commercial landlord, Craig. My saving grace was that he advertised a trailer full of used tires on Craigslist and sold the entire load to people who were in dire need of used tires. This bailed me out financially when I needed it most.

Also, I really have to give credit to Pastor Jim and his wife, Wendy. When I was at my peak of experiencing tangential thoughts, they kicked in and made phone calls to the Lebanon VAMC, thus making the right connection for me. Without Jim, I would have been sleeping in a snowbank.

At this point in my life, my teaching career was over, and my first stint as an independent businessperson had been flushed down the tubes. I learned a lot through the whole experience, and I know I will stand firm, whoever my medical treatment team is now and in the future at any given VAMC. However, the saga was just about to begin on so many issues I was naïve about.

I have always considered myself to be somewhat of a financial whiz kid, but until things went fiscally south for me, I never realized how tough monetary issues are in today's financial communities. I didn't know right then how bad things could be for me financially, such as prematurely cashing in a ton of securities and investments and ending up owing the IRS a ton of money to this day. For once in my life, I was really clueless until "Dr. Tom Cruise" (Jo Barbar) recommended I take on a more complex issue and file for bankruptcy. The total debt I escaped from came to approximately $450,000. This was due to the fact that I had gone on several manic spending sprees. Even outside of my business, I was financially out of control. The question I was faced with was whether to fight or flee. Should I take on my debts myself, or let the legal system give me a fresh start in the world? I decided to swallow my pride and elect for bankruptcy. A few other people gave me their opinions, but the decision was ultimately mine. This was a true test of my ability to recover and think rationally again. I quickly learned that bankruptcy was a tool that worked for me. Although it is not required that a person in a position like mine file for bankruptcy, it certainly is something worth investigating if you ever find yourself in a similar position.

A lot of people are stymied by their finances and struggle with the issue of budgeting, which is something that could help them deal with bankruptcies. Most people have a difficult time making a realistic budget on their own. When I was dealing with my illness during that period, I was no exception. On many occasions, my expenses exceeded by revenues. I was not very good at exploring the financial options which might have kept me out of bankruptcy. I didn't start making a budget for myself until my business was too far gone in the wrong direction, and I was in danger of losing my house because I didn't include my mortgage payment in my daily expenses. I just loaded one stress factor after another on myself.

To remedy my situation, one of the first things I did was contact a consumer credit counselor in Lancaster, PA to help me get my personal affairs back in order. A consumer credit counselor can help you prepare a budget that will send you back in the right direction. In my case, I was too far gone. My problem was that I didn't catch the easy mistakes right away, so when I did find the right help, it was too late.

At that time, things were whirling a million miles a minute for me. What was accepted as modern-day financial reform and practice didn't seem to apply to me. Somehow, a large number of debt collectors managed to get ahold of my personal phone number, so my time at home became a living nightmare. I was slow to get a lawyer involved because at that point I thought I could manage things with my own personal savvy (like I handled my business). A lot of debt collectors called me, trying to sell me debt consolidation loans. I approached these types of loans with a high degree of skepticism, which was good, because I discovered that these types of loans are like playing double jeopardy with your personal financial situations. I clearly learned that if a person didn't understand the terms, interest rates, and fees associated with a loan, it was a bad investment. I realized that a debt consolidation loan would just be a delay in positioning me for the inevitable. I wanted to get free of debt without incurring a balloon payment. A home equity loan was not an option for me, either, since I had absolutely no equity in my house, and I was probably going into foreclosure along with bankruptcy.

If you elect to participate in a program where a debt service negotiates with your creditors or makes payments on your behalf, be sure to understand whether or not that service will lower the amount you owe, plus the interest rate. If this is not the case, the plan in all likelihood will fail. Some debt counselors confine themselves to dealing with your unsecured commercial creditors, excluding your obligation for non-dischargeable child support, unpaid taxes, and automobile loans. In effect, those debt counselors ignore the debts that are more important, while your money goes to creditors whose claims could be discharged in bankruptcy.

Bankruptcy usually results because people have problems paying their debts. They are threatened with garnishment of wages, fore-closures, or repossessions. Considering bankruptcy is not the easiest decision to make, but it may be the most plausible to help you deal with your financial problems.

You have the right under federal law to file for bankruptcy relief from your creditors. Bankruptcy is a legal proceeding in which you can get a fresh financial start. It can also be very useful and effective in resolving problems in many cases. However, time is everything in filing for bankruptcy relief.

There are many things that bankruptcy can do, such as eliminate the legal obligation to pay most, or all, of your debts. This is called a "discharge of debts." Bankruptcy can also stop foreclosures on your home and allow you to catch up on missed payments. It may also stop foreclosures on a car or other property, or in some situations, force the creditors to return the property even after it has been repossessed. However, there are a few things bankruptcy can't do, such as discharging debts which arise after the bankruptcy has been filed. Bankruptcies can't discharge debts such as child support, alimony, divorce-related costs, most student loans, or criminal fines.

Under legal advice, I ended up taking out a Chapter 7 bankruptcy. A Chapter 7 is known as a "fresh start" bankruptcy, or liquidation. Your debts are discharged (cancelled), but you must give up any nonexempt property to the trustee to pay your creditors. In my case I didn't have any. As soon as you file for a Chapter 7 bankruptcy, you will be protected from credit agency harassment. Creditors are forbidden to call you once proceedings have started. However, the time it takes to re-establish your credit after filing for bankruptcy is long and difficult. Don't lose faith, though. The key to thinking smart from this point forward is managing your credit better (I really need to follow my own advice on that one). A word of advice: positive things will come in due time. This is proven experience from lessons I've learned.

How I pulled myself out of that particular pit of despair, I will never know. I can only attribute it to my lawyer and my medical treatment team at the Lebanon VAMC. Thanks to them, I was able to turn my life around. My lawyers got me through the bankruptcy, and my medical treatment team handled everything that said "medical" on it. Once again, "Dr. Tom Cruise" (Jo Barbar) was the man of the hour. I hardly ever say thank you to anyone except my mother, but this time I will gladly tip my hat to the highly trained professionals of the Lebanon VAMC and of course my lawyer.

My medical troubles at this time were beginning

to plague me once again. It appeared that through the end of 2013 I was still having problems with cognitive deficits which may have been due to viral encephalitis. I remember many a day when I would beg for my headaches to stop and for my memory to start working again. I was not at ease with myself. Every time I tried to concentrate, it was a losing battle. I was starting to lose faith in the system. For once my executive research abilities couldn't find the correct answers, plus the intolerable pain I was in made me a complete jerk to be around. I was very self-centered during that period. Although I knew there were many veterans ahead of me on the list for the required treatment as well, I refused to let my voice go unheard.

I had grown to hate the year 2013 with a passion. Whether my pain was due to the malingering effects of my post-concussion syndrome or the remnants of viral encephalitis, I didn't know. I still hated life. I felt that since the government, along with my own clumsy efforts, had been chasing my problems since 1991, there was little hope for my situation right then. I didn't know what I had ever done to be consigned to this eternal damnation. How much I should bring to bear on my shoulders, I didn't know.

Two weeks into the New Year, I finally had a chance to smile for a change. For the first time in almost three years, I thought I just might have it together for the first time. This took place after I agreed to cognitive therapy at the Hershey Medical Center. This was exactly the feeling of completeness I had been waiting for: a chance to be whole again, to be reunited with what my soul had lost.

When I had arrived at the Neuro-science clinic of the Hershey Medical Center in January of 2014, I really wasn't sure of myself right then. If this was going to be just another psychiatric intake session, I felt like it was going to be a waste of my time. As I sat in the examination room for two hours, that was precisely how I felt. After so many different intake sessions from all around the world, I wondered how long I could keep the story straight. Actually, I thought we were going for a record at that point. After waiting for such a long period of time, frustration became the name of the game, yet I knew this visit was for my benefit. That meeting with the neuropsychiatrist was probably the best thing that could ever happen to me at that point in my life.

Even though I was deeply angered about having to wait so long, the neuropsychiatrist turned out to be a very cool and understanding person. This was true, even though I was in a high degree of anticipation that day, and the facts didn't deviate too much from any other physician's intake session, since I was the one giving the story for the umpteenth time.

Just to reiterate my story as part of the intake interview, I told her I suffered a concussion in 1991 while on active duty in the US Army. This happened within seconds of a car wreck. I suffered symptoms of headache, impaired memory, and problems with higher executive functions, such as emotional intelligence and critical thinking. Despite that, I was able to work and provide for myself until 2010, when I suffered increased stress while losing my business due to hypomanic behavior. Subsequently, I was also recovering from viral encephalitis, which occurred in 2007. My bipolar behavior was controlled by 2010, but I still suffered from cognitive impairment and was incapable of concentrating and learning new things. One of the primary reasons I had become more aggressive in working with the Lebanon VAMC and in seeking help from the Hershey Medical Center was so that I could obtain therapy for helping me overcome my cognitive deficits and hopefully return to work.

Hershey AND Beyond

Believe it or not, despite all the agony and torture I had been through, I was willing to go back to work. Regardless of the negate innuendoes sent my way by so many people, whether due to the fact I was lazy or bipolar, I still wanted to work. My last neuro-psych evaluation done at Lebanon VAMC had revealed an average IQ and mild slowing of what is called serial processing speed or being able to complete one task before starting another one. My working memory (short-term memory) was at the first percentile, while my delayed memory (more long-term) was at the 21st percentile—all this as a result of the encephalitis. Yet I was still willing to go back to work! I probably should have been classified as a fool right then.

At that point I had no idea how neuroscience or speech therapy might be able to help me recapture my cognitive skills, but with a degree of optimism I was willing to try. After suffering for almost seven years from encephalitis, without anybody coming up with a solution as to how to treat it, I felt I was at the end of my rope. I thought my misery had no end in sight. However, somewhere or somehow, I had faith in the medical system that I might find the internal fortitude I needed to excel and to survive. I needed to have peace within myself once and for all, whether it be teaching as an adjunct professor once again or writing books. I was struggling to find a new identity. Somewhere between the Lebanon VAMC and the Hershey Medical Center, I felt that I would gain peace of mind once and for all.

Every day that I approached cognitive therapy, I did so with a high degree of anticipation, due to the fact that I didn't know what to expect initially, especially in the realm of self-improvement. I set my personal standards higher and higher with each session. I was running on pure adrenaline, though, primarily because I was afraid of failure.

In one of my earliest sessions, I was introduced to circumlocution as a strategy for dealing with periods of anomia (not being able to think of the names of things). Circumlocution included describing something by means of its category, function, location (where it might be found), or its size or shape. The object couldn't be named in conversation. At first, I was not sure what this strategy was, but after a high degree of repetition, I began to see its usefulness.

As a result of THIS strategy, my long-term goals are

to improve my cognitive linguistic skills and language functions. This is a milestone I don't think I have yet achieved, but I am very much aware of the goals I have set for myself and don't expect anything lower than what I feel I can accomplish.

At that point, I began to wonder if increasing my overall cognitive skills by twenty-five percent long term might seem a little bit beyond my reach, but as I sit here now and cross-examine myself, I think I can establish complete independence without too much difficulty.

My clinician has pointed out that from session to session I have been demonstrating good carryover of the strategies taught for memory and organization. She also has noticed that I have been using these new learned strategies very quickly in day-to-day functioning.

During training activities on the computer, I have demonstrated some degree of difficulty integrating attention and memory alongside motor and computer skills. (No big mystery on that one.) Psycho-motor skills were never one of my strong skills (and still aren't), as a result of the deficiencies suffered from viral encephalitis.

So many days went by in rehabilitation where I felt completely stymied and thought that success would permanently elude me.

Despite the negative feelings I have occasionally had about my progress, my clinician has pointed out that I have been demonstrating good carryover of strategies for memory and organization on a daily basis. I have begun to realize their importance every day and have begun to see the value in using these strategies in day-to-day functioning and integrating all the new psycho-motor skills I have learned through rehabilitation. I just thought to myself that this time I would not be denied, even though in a cognitive way I would have to learn how to walk before I could run.

As a result of my cognitive training, I quickly ascertained why I had opted out of law school and had gone on to pursue my MBA instead. My clinician asked me to complete a deductive puzzle. (Just another reason to become intellectually frustrated, or so it seemed.) I had completed the same puzzle the previous day but had required assistance. Surprisingly enough, the following day I completed the very same puzzle in a timely manner, with one hundred percent accuracy. I was shocked at my own performance.

Then came the real trick—to complete a second puzzle the following day, with no verbal cueing. Could I do that? Not even close. I needed my clinician's assistance in order for me to complete the task, which left me completely befuddled from the get-go.

So here I stand, poised for my next adventure.